A Seer and Science Topple Evolution

By
Thomas G. Davies

TEACH Services, Inc.
New York

2006 07 08 09 10 11 12 · 5 4 3 2 1

Copyright © 2006 TEACH Services, Inc.
ISBN-13: 978-1-57258-423-5
ISBN-10: 1-57258-423-8
Library of Congress Control Number: 2006923444

Published by

TEACH Services, Inc.
www.TEACHServices.com

Contents

Trade Tower Disaster Long Ago Forseen!

Stupendously, reader, an insightful nineteenth century seer foresaw a seeming replica of the New York Trade Tower disaster—listen!

> On one occasion, when in New York City, I was in the night season called upon to behold buildings rising story after story toward heaven. These buildings were warranted to be fireproof, and they were erected to glorify their owners and builders. Higher and still higher these buildings rose, and in them the most costly material was used. Those to whom these buildings belonged were not asking themselves: "How can we best glorify God?"
>
> The scene that next passed before me was an alarm of fire. Men looked at the lofty and supposedly fireproof buildings and said: "They are perfectly safe." But these buildings were consumed as if made of pitch. The fire engines could do nothing to stay the destruction. The firemen were unable to operate the fire engines.[1]

Stupendous, indeed, reader—that such a scene could have been seen and described so long ago with such accuracy as to the actual happening! And notice that this was not the work of some crystal-ball-gazing psychic—for it was revealed while the seer was normally asleep at night.

And so naturally, we want to know just who this insightful seer or prophet is—and fortunately, there is one who can satisfyingly enlighten us as to it all—one Rene Noorbergen by name. And for many, reader, that name makes real sense. Sense in that this popular author of a few years back had made it his work to study into and with, and write concerning, the then-popular and well known psychics of the day.

And after all that indepth investigation, reader, this man's plain intelligence made him admittingly write as follows.

> "James Bjornstad, author of *Twentieth Century Prophecy*, dealing with the prophetic phenomena as displayed by Edward Cayce and Jeanne Dixon, has made a number of interesting comparisons between the abilities of these two psychics and the Biblical requirements for a true prophet.
>
> His conclusion, based strictly on Biblical references, is for them truly devastating! Comparing all...one arrives at the conclusion that all psychic mediums...without exception not only violate many basic Biblical principles but also more often than not act in stark contradiction to the biblical norms for a true prophet.[2]

But what a refreshing difference, reader, this exhaustive researcher found as he fortunately was led to look into the prophetic experience of the author of our opening New York revelation. Here he read, not just one, but many prophecies divulged over many long years, that he could see—unlike the psychic's oft-failing prognostications—could not have been closer to fact!

And along with the long-ago-given New York revelation, Noorbergen was astounded with the accuracy of an outstanding but senses-jarring one given not long before the end of her eighty-seven years came to an end. Listen, reader, as we take the abridged high points of his following account thereof.

Ellen G. White had seen the destruction of San Francisco pass before her as early as 1902, when she warned as follows. "Not long hence these cities will suffer under the judgements of God. San Francisco and Oakland are becoming as Sodom and Gomorrah, and the Lord will visit them in wrath."

A year passed during which time many of her inspired counsels were received and heeded, but San Francisco and Oakland remained under the waiting axe of the Eternal Judge. Not only Ellen White, but others also seemed to sense that this great city of the West was rapidly approaching a point of no return in a race to reach the absolute summit of immorality!

A flood of revival meetings, religious crusades and scores of independent Bible workers begged the sinking city to repent—but time went on, and nothing changed.

Ellen White's anxiety increased. And during the Spring of 1906 she received the final vision that spelled out doom for the debauched city. She related:

There passed before me a most distressing representation.

During a vision of the night, I stood on an eminence from which I could see houses shaken like a reed in the wind. Buildings, great and small, were falling to the ground. Pleasure resorts, theaters, hotels, and the homes of the wealthy were shaken and shattered. Many lives were blotted out of existence, and the air was filled with the shrieks of the injured and the terrified.

The destroying angels of God were at work. One touch, and buildings so thoroughly constructed that men regarded them as secure against every danger, quickly became heaps of rubbish. There was no assurance of safety in any place. The awfulness of the scenes that passed before me I cannot find words to describe.

The day of the quake, Ellen White, enroute to fill a speaking engagement in Los Angeles, suddenly stopped. A newsboy's high-pitched voice suddenly brought back the memory of the visions she had received in clear and vivid detail about the destruction of San Francisco.

"San Francisco destroyed by earthquake!" he screamed excitedly. "San Francisco destroyed by earthquake—the city's going up in flames!" And buying a paper, with a heavy heart Ellen began to read the sad account. A prophecy had literally been fulfilled. And the prophet wept.[3]

So here we see two prophecies of a local nature, reader, that were completely fulfilled as foretold. But author Noorbergen relates another of this insightful prophet's prophecies that also includes our total dying old planet.

As we again thus take the high points as follows, listen! "At the rate he is going, man could consume and pollute his way to oblivion in the near future!" That is the gloomy prediction voiced by leading ecologist Dr. Kenneth Watt of the University of California.

Basing his pessimistic assertion on the alarming rate at which our modern technological society is consuming the planet's limited natural resources—the over-population, the continuing pollution of the earth and atmosphere, and the gross neglect of what still remains—he felt that man is actually preparing the planet for total extinction! And, most responsible scientists now agree with this dire possibility.

But, when this "prophet of destiny" lived from 1827 on, the threat of such pollution was, of course, unheard of. And the far-fetched idea that man could some day be accused of killing his own planet would then have been considered ludicrous. But, in her visions prior to 1890, she was shown the havoc man would indeed create on this planet. And typically, she chronicled all such in warning to mankind.

Therein, she declared:

> In the future, the condition of things in the cities will grow more and more objectionable. From the standpoint of health, the smoke and dust (smog) of the cities are very objectionable. The physical surroundings in the cities are often a peril to health. The constant liability of contact with disease (SARS, "superbugs"), the prevalence of foul air, impure water and food, poisonous gases (carbon dioxide), are some of the many evils to be met there.
>
> The time is coming erelong when all who wish to avoid the sights and sounds of evil, will move into the country. For wickedness and corruption will increase to such a degree that the very atmosphere of the cities will seem polluted. Satan is working in the atmosphere and is poisoning it. And here we are dependent upon God for our lives, both present and eternal. Said the apostle John in Revelation 11:18: "And the nations were angry and Thy wrath has come...that Thou shouldst destroy them which destroy the earth."[4]

How very accurate an early-given prophetic picture of just such right today, reader! And this all above back in those horse and buggy days when the cities were still midgets beside those of today and such as foretold was never dreamed of.

Except, that is, that this servant of the Lord throughout her seventy long years of such ministry extensively travelled and spoke thereon, among other subjects , continent-wide. And this much by appointment and well covered by reporters and columnists. This, as she lectured to often huge audiences, beside having her messages and prolific writings spread even worldwide in newspapers, magazines, pamphlets, and books.

And, another type of "polluting", reader, that comes closer home to us yet, was going on in another area, and which she similarly addressed, the high points of author Noorbergen's coverage of such being as follows.

Listen:

> In June, 1863, Ellen White was publicly taken away in vision and which lasted upward of an hour. The very next day she began to write down that revealed to her. Prior to this, that shown her had mainly to do with the religious field.
>
> However, with all the world living, or better, surviving, in an age when sub-human treatment of sickness was erroneously regarded as medical aid, the time was now ripe for health-related counsel and medical insight. And, fortunately, this vision did indeed refer insightfully to just that.
>
> Indeed, such could not have been given at a more appropriate time in history. For, misguided medical practice had reached a peak of intense controversy due to the ignorance and arrogance of its varied practitioners. This especially to do with the ungrounded importance the profession attached to its two main methods of treatment. These were "bleeding", often to the point of death, and, the over-reliance on harsh drugs and opiates.
>
> Regarding such, Dr. J. H. Kellog said in 1876: "Twenty years ago, when a man had a fever, the doctors thought that he had too much vitality and life, and so they bled him, purged him, and literally poisoned him, with calomel, blue mass, and sundry other such poisons, thus killing him little by little." Not knowing the underlying causes of disease, all they did was try to treat the symptoms.
>
> But now, fortunately, this timely vision's indepth insights exposed highly advanced and revolutionary new information. This all dealing with nutrition, health principles, disease treatment, as well as a

wealth of scientific data unknown back in Ellen White's day.[5]

And, reader, this all so medically foundational and sensibly sound as to be completely accepted in our medically-advanced day! This including by knowledge-able people in high places. For trite example, listen as follows to excerpts from the media-presented testimo-nial of the distinguished columnist-broadcaster Paul Harvey as he typically tells "the rest of the story" hereon.

> Once upon a time, a hundred years ago, there lived a young lady named Ellen Harmon White. She was frail as a child—injured by a playmate—so completed only grammar school, and had no technical training, yet lived to write scores of articles and numerous books, including on the subject of healthful living.

> Now remember, this was in the days when doctors were blood-letting and performing surgery with unwashed hands. This was an era of medical ignorance bordering on barbarism! Yet, Ellen White wrote with such profound understanding on, among many others, the subject of nutrition, that all but two of the many revolutionary principles she espoused, have to date been scientifically established.

> Professor of Nutrition, Dr. Clive MacKay of Cornell University asserted: "How much better health the average American might enjoy if he had but followed the teachings of Mrs. White!" So perhaps best that we should simply read some of what she taught, as follows. example: "The oil, as eaten in the olive, is far preferable to animal oil or fat." Today, of course, we know all about cholesterol! (LDL and transfats too!)

> She knew and so stated: "Fine flour white bread—the staple back then—is lacking in nutritive elements to be found in bread made from the whole wheat." Today, of course, we have "enriched" our white bread. Also, she wrote: "Do not eat largely of

salt" (in a day when much was thus preserved). Now we know we should keep our sodium intake low.

Further, she wrote whole articles on the importance of not overeating and of not becoming overweight, and, "to eat no more than is required to satisfy hunger" (important for weight maintenance, and, for weight reduction without special diets!). A long time ago, before we learned about TV snacks, Mrs. White wisely wrote: "After irregular eating, when children come to the table, they then do not relish wholesome food; their appetites crave rather that which is hurtful to them" ("junk food!") And she further urged for health: "Pure air, sunlight, abstemiousness, rest, exercise, and trust." Ellen White was indeed ahead of her time![6]

How natural, reader—though often not wanting to be admitted—that what we ingest has much to do with our general health. And Mrs. White, as Paul Harvey showed, had much to say on that matter. Indeed, a whole book has been compiled from such wise advance advice, entitled *Counsels On Diet and Foods*.

And in that and other advice presented, reader, she even cautions about today's perhaps most dreaded disease, cancer—advising that, as we now know, it can be induced by such common things as cancer-laden meats, harsh chemicals and drugs, and pollutants.

And, concerning cancer and other dire diseases, in her continent-wide crusade for betterment of health, she even attacked, away back then, a leading cancer-causing pollutant—tobacco smoking. Indeed, after her health vision, as early as 1864, she warned as follows. So listen as author Noorbergen applies her testimonials.

Tobacco is a poison of the most deceitful and malignant kind, having an exciting, then paralyzing influence upon the nerves of the body. It is all the more dangerous because its effects upon the system are so slow and at first scarcely perceivable. Multitudes have fallen victim to its poisonous influence. They have surely murdered themselves by this slow-acting poison.

Can you imagine the ridicule to which Mrs. White was exposed, when she publicly made these statements? This, at a time when the medical world regarded and advocated tobacco and cigar smoke as an effective cure for lung diseases! Then, many a doctor advocated such as this advice: "the patient should frequently draw in the breath freely, so that the internal surface of the air vessels may be exposed to the action of the smoke vapor!"

Whereas, in 1957, scientists of the American Cancer Society and the American Heart Association declared as follows. "The sum total of scientific evidence has established beyond a reasonable doubt that cigarette smoking is a causative factor in the rapidly increasing incidence of human carcinoma of the lung." So science discovered this fact a century after this danger had been revealed to Ellen White.[7]

And on top of this, reader—beside her far-in-advance warning concerning such prenatal influences on the fetus—listen to her warning in her relevant writings regarding second-hand smoke, given long years before such was even known!

Women and children suffer from having to breathe the atmosphere that has been polluted by the tobacco user. Those having to live in this atmosphere will always be ailing (pets too, now the scientists advise). And the lungs of infants become diseased by inhaling it. Their system is filled thus with poison and they waste away. Then the bereaved parents wonder concerning "the mysterious providence of God" which has supposedly so cruelly afflicted them!

No wonder columnist Paul Harvey, reader, further warningly wrote as follows.

> Mrs. White also wrote "Tobacco is a slow, insidious, and most malignant poison. It is all the more dangerous because its effects are slow and at first hardly perceptible." So, divinely inspired or not, Ellen White was indeed ahead of her time! Thus we are led to wonder if there are additional recommendations which this remarkable woman urged upon us which we have, so far, ignored.[8]

The word "ignored" was used advisedly, reader, because not being "done in a corner", as mentioned, such was well publicized even nation-wide. And that this was so, was manifestly aired in the following editorial a while back in none other than *The Saturday Evening Post*.

Listen:

> Long before nutrition achieved the status of a full-fledged science, an extraordinary woman named Ellen G. White, was instructing church members in the basic concepts of healthful living.

> It wasn't alone that she denounced the use of alcohol and tobacco and addictive drugs. Or even that she wrote a century ago that "tobacco is a slow, insidious, and most malignant poison" that was most remarkable. For, even more remarkable for back then, were her insistence on a well-balanced diet, even before the phrase was heard of.

> Her emphasis on natural foods in season when possible; her denunciation of meat consumption, and especially of animal fats, a century before cholesterol and polyunsaturated became popular words was remarkable. As also were her rejection of refined food, particularly white flour and sugar, before scientists suspected there were health connections and vitamins that could be destroyed by the refining

processes. While now it is verified that fine-flour bread is lacking nutritive elements found in bread made from the whole grain and the lack of which can cause unhealthful conditions.

She also back then taught: "Those who eat flesh meat are but eating grains and vegetables at second hand; for the animal receives from such, nutrition producing its growth. The life from the animal eaten passes on to the eater. How much better to get it directly, by eating the foods God originally provided for our use" (fruits, nuts, grains, vegetables—Genesis 1:29, 30, 3:19).

Although not prohibited, many members abstain from eating flesh foods, which has had significant results, as many scientific studies have revealed. One main result is that this has supplied the world at large with helpful and impressive medical health statistics. This, based upon the eminent fact that members are shown thus to be the healthiest and long-living people, by and large, in the country.

Such findings and statistics have caused many non-members using their many medical and educational institutions worldwide, to also choose to become vegetarians. An added bonus to this, of course, is that for those who follow such a lifestyle, there is the shown incidence of having much less heart attacks and cancer along with other debilitating afflictions and diseases.

And all of this, because, they say by Providence, seventeen year old Ellen Harmon, later White, was given and accepted the prophetic gift with its accompanying visions.

Now out of this special instruction and guidance, has come the rapid growth of a vast worldwide network of institutions and work. And from her primary health vision in 1863 arose the then world-famous Battle Creek Sanitarium under the renowned Dr. John Harvey Kellog. While from brother W. K. Kellog came the world's first "cornflakes" and the breakfast cereal industry.

And on her death at the ripe age then of 88, in St. Helena, California, Mrs. White's gift had left 53 full-length books on every conceivable subject needed for wholesome living both physically and spiritually. Her some 25 million words, 100,000 handwritten pages, 5,000 articles, and reams of personal letters to individuals, spoke for themselves by the fruitage they manifestly bore. And this was partly seen in the tens of millions of her books sold and circulated worldwide, making her one of the most prolific and best-selling authors of all time.[9]

What a track record, reader! Surely the "proof of the pudding", and of the prophet. And pertinently hereon, author Noorbergen, in verification, gives a scriptural ten-point list of prophetic qualifications, showing she fulfilled them all. Now most of these requirements are such as to be expected, such as that the prophet will be a good and godly person and that his or her prophecies will be fulfilled as specified.

However, reader, there is one totally unusual, yes, otherworldly such, that can and does set the God-given prophet totally and unequivocally apart from the pseudo-psychics. This, no doubt being a God-given testimonial and proof that will help even the gainsayers and doubters to be led to believe, if they will.

And author Noorbergen relates a scriptural illustration thereof, reader, by way of verification. Listen: "A classic example of this is found in Daniel 10:5–19, where this old-time prophet related his own experience when a mysterious being appeared to him when in vision. These reactions exhibit a similarity to those experienced by Ellen White, and are as follows.

1. A glorious being appeared to Daniel

2. he lost his strength and fell into a deep sleep face downward

3. He heard the voice of the being speaking to him

4. When the being touched him, he rose to his hands and knees

5. He was at first unable to speak, but the being touched his lips so he could

6. Remarkably, he did not breathe!

7. He was then strengthened for the vision.[10]

An astounding circumstance, reader—that in vision the prophet did not breathe!—certainly a most verifying God-given and miraculous proof of the genuineness thereof. And concerning the undisputable fact that such was the case with Ellen White, author Noorbergen illustrates as follows.

Listen!:

> Numerous eyewitness accounts covering every aspect of Mrs. White's being in vision, are among the thousands of documents filed away in the archives of the Mrs. E. G. White estate. Therein, by way of example, Martha Amadon, a close associate of Mrs. White, and who witnessed many of her visions, stated as follows.

> As one who has frequently observed Mrs. White in vision, I saw that her eyes were open, but that there was no breathing. There were however, graceful movements expressive of what she was envisioning. But, at the same time, it was impossible for anyone to move her hands and arms. She sometimes uttered words expressing the nature of what she was seeing. Then, on coming out of vision, as she then took her first breath, when she apparently lost sight of heavenly light, she would exclaim with a sigh, "Dark", after which she lay limp for a time.

And a professional account, given by Dr. M. G. Kellog, was as follows.

On this occasion, Mrs. White was in vision for about half an hour. The occasion was that of a prayer meeting, when we besought God to bless the meeting with His presence. Suddenly, as Mrs. White went into vision, everyone felt the presence and power of God and His Spirit resting mightily upon us.

With this, brother White informed the audience that Mrs. White was in vision. After stating by way of authentication that she did not breathe when in vision, he invited anyone to come and examine her for verification.

Then Dr. Drummond, a First Day Adventist physician and preacher, who had formerly declared her visions to be of mesmeric origin and that he himself could put her into one, came forward. Examining her by using a mirror to test for breath, he exclaimed: "Indeed, she does not breathe!"

And this was authenticated in a similar occasion. This was that a Dr. Brown, a spiritualistic physician of Parkville, Michigan, had stated openly that she was simply experiencing a form of spiritualistic mediumship. Further, that he wished for an opportunity to examine her while in vision, declaring that he could control her therein. Well, that occasion just happened to come about when Mrs. White spoke at a meeting in Parkville, January 12, 1861.

At the close of this meeting, Mrs. White was taken off in vision. And responding now to brother White's invitation to come and examine her, this Dr. Brown, who just happened to be present, came up and made an examination of her state. But, the eyewitness account asserts, "Before Dr. Brown had a chance to examine further, he started to shake and turned pale. As brother White asked what he had to report as to his findings, he retorted: "She does not breathe!"

The abashed doctor then quickly made his way toward the door. But, some exclaimed, "Go back doctor, and as you have claimed, bring her out of vision." But when asked just what her state was in vision, grasping the door knob, he gasped, "God only knows—let me out of here!"[11]

No, reader, an all-wise God saw fit to dramatically separate between the genuine and the counterfeit. He separated between the devil's children of darkness and His children of light in this way that left no doubt as to which it was. For, though the devil can indeed work seeming miracles—here, in this matter of God's prophets not breathing while in vision, is one miracle even the powerful devil himself cannot duplicate!

And well does author Noorbergen state:

> And fortunate indeed is this at a time when more than 10,000 professional astrologers control the daily activities of some 40 million people in the United States through some 1,200 daily astrology columns and 2,350 horoscope computers; when roughly 140,000 fortune-tellers, mediums, clairvoyants, and psychic seers, have created a 42 million dollar-a-year business. Yes, when three major universities offer credit courses in witchcraft, magic, astrology, and sorcery, how necessary to have a foolproof method to separate the psychics from the prophets.[12]

Yes, reader, we can trust and thank a more than good God that He gives us every good assist and reason to savingly believe. But, not only did He give us this foolproof assist as described, but, as seen, He also gave His servant many prophetic insights that have been and are confirmingly being fulfilled to further encourage and help us to believe.

Not only past occurrences, reader, but ones being fulfilled before our startled eyes right today. For trite example, as follows, listen as from her *"Great Contro-versy"* vision given her in 1858, Ellen White startlingly describes!

> Satan appears as a benefactor of the race, healing (remember, he works through people he controls—in this case perhaps "faith-healers", New Agers, etc.) the diseases of the people, and professing to present a new and more exalted system of religious faith; but at the same time, he works as a destroyer...
>
> Satan delights in war, for, it excites the worst passions of the soul, and then sweeps into eternity its victims steeped in vice and blood. So it is his object to incite the nations to war against one another; for he can thus divert the minds of the people from the work of preparation to stand in the day of God.[13]

> The tempest is coming, and we must get ready for its fury by having repentance toward God and faith toward our Lord Jesus Christ...We shall see troubles on all sides. Thousands of ships will be hurled into the depths of the sea. Navies will go down, and human lives will be sacrificed by the millions (what but the two Great World Wars could have been envisioned?!).
>
> Fires will break out unexpectedly and no human effort will be able to quench them. The palaces (mansions!) of earth will be swept away in the fury of the flames.
>
> Disasters by rail will become more and more frequent; confusion, collision, and death without a moment's warning will occur on the great lines of travel (unknown in her horse and buggy days!). The end is near, probation is closing. Oh, let us seek the Lord while He may be found.[14]

It isn't hard to indeed believe her assertion the end is near, reader. And this also as seeing her following enlightenment, we recall how it all has been, and is, ominously and destructively happening right now in our day.

Listen!:

> Satan works through the elements also to gather his harvest of unprepared souls. He has studied the laboratories of nature, and he uses all his power to control the elements as far as God allows...It is God that shields His creatures, and hedges them in from the power of the destroyer...

> While appearing (through his agents) to the children of men as a great physician who can heal all their maladies, he will bring disease (SARS, AIDS, West Nile, Asian Flu, BSE Mad Cow Disease, etc!) and disaster, until populous cities are reduced to ruin and desolation.

> Even now Satan is at work. In accidents and calamities by sea and by land, in great conflagrations, in fierce tornadoes and terrific hail storms, in tempests, floods, cyclones (hurricanes), tidal waves (tsunamis!), and earthquakes, in every place and in a thousand forms, Satan is exercising his power.

> He sweeps away the ripening harvest, and famine and distress follow. He imparts to the air a deadly taint, and thousands perish by the pestilence. These visitations are to become more and more frequent and disastrous. Destruction will be upon both man and beast.[15]

Just like watching or reading today's news, reader!—yet, obviously by providence, warningly given many long years ago. As also was the light as to who this great adversary of God and man was, Satan by name, which, in the original, means just that—adversary. And author Noorbergen sketches what Ellen White, away back in her 1858 *Great Controversy* vision was shown and related hereon.

As we see the high points, listen!:

She related that concerning the matter of the great controversy between Christ and Satan, she was instructed to write it out for publication. This time Ellen was transported into a time before and beyond that of recorded history and was made witness to the War in Heaven (as described in Revelation 12), and the rebellion and fall of Lucifer.

She wrote:

The Lord has shown me that Satan, then Lucifer, was once an honored angel in heaven, and next in position to Christ. But when God said to His Son, 'Let us make man in Our image', Satan became jealous of Jesus. He also wished to be consulted concerning the formation of man, and, because he was not, he was filled with envy, jealousy, and hatred. For, he desired to receive the highest honors in heaven next to God.

Until this time, all heaven had been in order, harmony, and perfect subjection to the government of God. Now all heaven seemed in commotion. There was contention among the angels. Lucifer and his duped sympathizers were striving to reform the very government of God. They rebelled against the authority of the Son.

Then, all the heavenly host were summoned to appear before the Father to have each case decided. Then it was determined that Lucifer, now Satan the adversary, should be expelled from heaven with all the angels who had joined him in the rebellion. Then there was war in heaven, but the good and true angels prevailed, and Satan, with his followers, was driven from heaven (as plainly recorded in Revelation 12).

Now Satan's malice and hatred began to be manifest. He consulted with his angels, and a plan was laid to still work against God's government. And when Adam and Eve were placed in the beautiful garden, Satan was laying plans to destroy them. It was decided that Satan should assume another form and pretend an interest in man. Then he would insinuate against God's truthfulness and create doubt as to whether He really meant just what He said.

Satan commenced this work with Eve when she wandered from her husband. Next when she approached and lingered around the forbidden tree. Then, in listening to the tempter's voice, it resulted in her daring to question and doubt what God had said in forbidding to approach or eat from the tree.

Now, this done, Eve seeing that the tree was "pleasant to the eyes", she put forth her hand and ate of its fruit. Then she became jealous that God had withheld from them what apparently was for their good, and tempting Adam with it, he too ate. Thus Satan triumphed. He had made others too suffer by his fall. He had resultingly been shut out of heaven, and they out of Paradise.[16]

And sadly for us today, reader, that age-old battle between God and Satan, Good and Evil, continues with full, yes accelerating force! Dr. Billy Graham, in *Angels: God's Secret Agents*, puts the high points this way:

We live in a perpetual battlefield—the great War of the Ages continues to rage. The lines of battle press in ever more tightly about God's Own people. The wars among nations on earth are mere popgun affairs compared to the fierceness of battle in the spiritual, unseen world. This invisible spiritual conflict is waged around us incessantly and unremittingly.

Where the Lord works, Satan's forces hinder; where angel beings carry out their divine directives, the devils rage. All this comes about because the powers of darkness press their counterattack to recapture the ground...Satan has great power. He is cunning and clever, having set himself against God and His people. He will do everything in his power to hold people captive in sin and drag them down.[17]

And this warrior for God, reader, knows whereof he speaks, because, as the writer, he has in his ministry, had to wage personal battle with such. And thus, in *Peace With God*, he further warns as follows.

> The Bible that tells us over and over again of God's love, warns us constantly of the Devil who would come between us and God, the Devil who is ever waiting to ensnare men's souls. It warns: "Be sober, be vigilant; because your adversary the devil, as a roaring lion walks about, seeking whom he may devour" (1 Pet. 5:8).

> Yes, the Bible describes a personal devil who controls a host of demon spirits that attempt to dominate and control all human activity. It describes the devil as: "The prince of the power of the air, the spirit that now works in the children of disobedience" (Ephesians 2:2).

> So, don't doubt for a moment the existence of the Devil! He is very personal and he is very real! And, he is extremely clever! Look again at the front page of today's newspaper if you have any questions about the personality of the Devil. Switch on your local radio or television news if you feel you need concrete evidence!

> Yes, a struggle of infinitely greater magnitude is being waged in the world we cannot see. The wise of old knew this. They were aware that there is much that the human eye fails to discern and much to which the human ear is deaf. Modern man likes to feel that he "created" radio and television, that he made it possible to send audible sounds and visible images through open space. The truth is, of course, that these invisible waves, unknown to man, have always existed.

> Thus, what we see happening here on earth is but a reflection of the far vaster struggles between good and evil in the unseen realm. The apostle Paul warned: "We wrestle not against flesh and blood, but against principalities, against powers, against the rulers of the darkness of this world, against spiritual wickedness (org. wicked spirits) in high places" (Eph.6:12).

Yes, Paul recognized the dreaded enemy, the powerful foe of all mankind. Two overwhelming powers were clearly apparent to him. The power of good was pulling his mind and heart toward God, while the power of evil was trying to drag his body down into death and destruction. And you are caught between these two same forces: life and death. Choose God's way![18]

So, reader, plain that we wrestle against powers, and the prince of the power of the air, as God's holy Word warns. Power—a word used time and time again all through, as back in Ellen White's inspired depiction of all we face today. Recall: "Satan...uses all his power to control the elements"; "God hedges His creatures from the power of the destroyer; in every place and in a thousand forms, Satan is exercising his power."

And yet, reader—as with radio and television beams, unfortunately, we don't visibly see this power as it is at its malign work. Enlightened Billy Graham, recall, illustrated just why as he pertinently said:

Modern man likes to feel that he "created" radio and television, that he made it possible to send audible sounds and visible images through open space. The truth is, of course, that these waves, unknown (and unseen) to man, have always existed.

Simple as that, reader—as well said, there are, and always have been, "waves" or rays and beams of invisible power circling earth, and all through space. Beam-waves that man has only lately come to understand and use. Use in radio and television, yes, and in micro-waves as in your micro-wave oven in your kitchen; in the rays or beams or waves of the X-ray or proton-ray machine your doctors use; in the rays that automatically open doors you enter in the elevator or store, to pinpoint a few.

And though these various wave-rays cannot be seen, reader, still, as we see, they do have definite effect—good, or, bad. Just like the simple magnet, recall, that awed you so when young, mysteriously drew the iron to itself. Yes, it had a definite power and pull and resulting effect, didn't it. And this is one reason, perhaps, that scientists named this whole myriad-form spectrum in space, "the electromagnetic spectrum"—one that though invisible, definitely has visible, experienced effects.

In the *McGraw-Hill Encyclopedia of Science and Technology*, reader, under the article "light", on page 55 it says as follows.

> The electromagnetic spectrum is a broad band of radiant energy which extends over a range of wavelengths running from trillionths of inches to hundreds of miles...Arranged in order of increasing wavelength, the radiation making up the electromagnetic spectrum is termed, gamma rays, x-rays, ultraviolet rays, visible light rays, infrared rays, microwaves, radio waves, and very long electromagnetic waves.

And so, reader, as pointed out, one of its components is visible—the light-ray. In *The Weekender*, Nov. 5, 2004, astronomer Andrew Waring wrote on such as follows.

> Look in any high school textbook and it will tell you that what we perceive as light, is actually one part of the electromagnetic spectrum. One that runs from x-rays to gamma rays. Actually comprising a very narrow part of the spectrum, visible light is simply energy, made up of photons, or packets of energy that move in waves.

And just perhaps, reader, the Creator left this one form of electromagnetism energy visible, so that we could see that also invisible waves exist and have energy—power—such as the invisible but active power that heats and cooks in your microwave oven, for one of many examples. And further, as to the convincing power of light-rays paralleling the invisible ones, what a display of just such has God left us to more than convince us to that end—lightning!

And on this subject, reader, the above-quoted encyclopedia, under "Light", on page 73, says as follows.

> Lightning is an abrupt, high-current electric discharge (energy!) that occurs in the atmosphere of earth. It has a path length ranging from hundreds of feet to tens of miles. Lightning occurs in thunderstorms because vertical air motions and interactions between cloud particles cause a separation of positive and negative charges.
>
> About one third of all discharges are from cloud to ground, and this type of lightning is the primary hazard to people and objects...The return stroke is basically a very intense, positive wave of ionization (electricity) that propagates up the partially ionized leader channel into the cloud at a speed close to the speed of light...Positive discharges are often quite deleterious...The rapidly rising return stroke current heats the channel to a peak temperature near 55,000 degrees fahrenheit.

Wave-rays of energy-power of the first magnitude, indeed, reader! Electrical power that causes us to expect, then, that it would be normal that the rest of the wave-rays in the relative electromagnetic spectrum also are energized by electrical power that also has "power"-ful effects!—though of course hopefully in lesser degree.

And well does the author recall being as a youngster rudely introduced to the fact that this basic component of electricity does indeed have "powerful" effects. This in that his smartaleck older cousin, now in technical school and anxious to show off his learning, did the "teaching" of this fact.

For, as we went down the basement, we passed by one of the old-time light switches, the cover of which was easily removed. So doing so, the cousin touched one of the terminals and told me to do so—with no effect. Then he touched the other one, telling me to also—no effect again. Then, he told me to touch both together, the foolish doing of which, quickly introduced me to the power of electricity as it jolted up my arm, smacking into my throbbing elbow!

A hard lesson well learned, reader, to hopefully spare from more deleterious and possibly damaging such in future. Yes, a future that, as scientific investigation and experimentation have continued, has increasingly revealed the indeed "power"-full effects of electromagnetic power. Often malign effects that due to their deleterious effects have been and are more and more being warningly revealed.

For trite example, reader, listen to the warning given in a recent journalistic report as follows that came to hand.

> New evidence on the physiological impacts of the electromagnetic fields on humans, has led to well-founded fears. For, the data shows powerful effects of being near electromagnetic fields, such as those around electric power lines.
>
> Being only a few feet from outdoor electric power lines can trigger cancer (so at last the truth is being admitted, reader, over this long debated matter!)...The studies, done at Michigan State University, show that magnetic fields impact on immature red blood cells causing a genetic mutation (abnormal change) that can cause cancer.

"We are convinced that electromagnetic fields can bring about a biological effect relevant to cancer development," said James Trosko of Michigan State. And Hiroshi Yamasaki of the International Agency For Research in France agrees...Thus it indicates that electromagnetic fields (influences) are a real health risk.[19]

And all this only stands to reason, reader—for, we ourselves are "electromagnetic!" Just quickly comb your hair in the dark before a mirror to see that as the sparks fly! Yes, the medical dictionary relevantly advises as follows.

Brain—the portion of the vertebrate central nervous system that constitutes the organ of thought and neural coordination and includes all the higher nervous centers receiving stimuli from the sense organs, and interpreting and correlating them to formulate the motor impulses...Brain wave—rhythmic fluctuations of voltage between parts of the brain resulting in the flow of an electric current.

So, reader, we, like the one in our car, are essentially a "wet battery!" An electrical wet battery that can, then, be affected by electromagnetic power's radiation. For recent example, the Autumn 2003 *Newsletter of the Proton Treatment Center* (an advanced form similar to X-ray) in Loma Linda, California, well illustrated such as follows.

A radiobiology program led the NASA project to investigating the central nervous system responses to (electromagnetic) radiation. Astronauts in space face several health risks resulting from long-term exposure to ionizing radiation. It has long been recognized that cancer and cataracts are among these risks...to the central nervous system. This system controls the body's homeostasis mechanism by way of electrical networks.

And an August 2004 article in the *Reader's Digest*, reader, gives researcher's hints as to the why of the above, saying as follows.

> Researchers at McLean Hospital in Massachusetts were studying brain chemistry of bipolar people, using an MRI with a unique electromagnetic pulse sequence. Thus the patient's moods lifted...Researchers aren't sure why it works, but there is a possible link, for, nerves in the brain fire electrical pulses. So, exposing them to a particular magnetic field could change the way the pulses fire.

So, reader, by all this, we indeed can see that the exposure of humans to these electric wave-ray influences, can indeed have a definite effect—for good, or, for bad—depending who or what is impinging them and in what way—the bad, unfortunately, causing harmful mutations and physiological changes. On such, the above-quoted Proton Treatment Center newsletter that was quoted regarding astronaut's risks from exposure to ionizing radiation, goes on to exemplify as follows.

> The collaboration (of numerous researchers) focuses on measuring radiation-induced loss of component brain cells in a central nervous system area having to do with learning and memory. Prior work by others had focused on the formation of necrotic brain lesions following very large doses of radiation, but had not measured changes in cell populations with time...Now researchers will measure brain function and the evolution of changes through time. And EEGs will map spontaneous electrical activity (an "evolution", then, reader, that rather than being progressive, is regressive!).

Another goal is to measure changes in the molecules that underlie cell and systemic changes as biochemical actions of radiation. The most fundamental site of ionizing radiation damage is chromatin and its constituent DNA, which can restrict or reprogram cell functions. Therefore, investigators will measure the frequency and determine the structural spectrum of mutations in a particular gene.

So you notice, reader, that these mutating, evolving changes over time actually reprogram body cell functions by way of harmful mutations of the vital DNA of the genes—our biological make-up "maps." And since we are herein dealing with such vital matters of the very bases of life itself, we need to refresh ourself thereon and as to life's constituents, such as pinpointed by the above use of such terms as "cell, molecules, chromatin, DNA, genes" and the like.

So since "cell" is first mentioned, reader, we could let *Collins Concise Encyclopedia* apply as follows.

Cell: fundamental unit of living matter. Consists of mass of protoplasm bounded by a membrane. Usually contains central nucleus surrounded by cytoplasm, in which enzyme systems which control cell's metabolism are situasted. Cells reproduce themselves by various methods of division.

Further investigation by science, reader, reveals that our bodies contain about 100 trillion of these cells! And further that the above-mentioned nucleus contains 23 pairs of chromosomes, and which are filled with double-stranded coils of DNA, and which house the all-important, determinative genes.

And on the genes, the above encyclopedia says:

"Unit of hereditary material. Genes are arranged into linear sequence to form chromosomes, each gene occurring at a specific point thereon. Composed of DNA, changes in structure of DNA cause mutation of genes, leading to changes in inheritable characteristics"

(more regressive "evolution", reader!)

And the complexity of the human body is further realized as we see that science reveals that there are roughly a hundred thousand of these genes packed into the cell's DNA. And the gene's main function is shown to be that it contains operable instructions as to the body's makeup. Further, that the DNA's double helix is a sort of winding molecular ladder, three billion rungs long! And that a specific gene can be a segment of DNA that is as short as a thousand rungs, or, as long as several hundred thousand rungs. Little wonder inspiration, reader, said that we are "fearfully and wonderfully" formed!

And in *The Way of the Cell,* scientist Franklin Harold, adds relative insight on our above considerations on the complicity of electrical power herein, as follows. Listen:

> Metabolism requires energy, and energy is provided by electrical power generated by the cell. An alternative energy source is also available, if required...The work of the molecules and proteins within the cell, is encoded in the genes thereof. It is estimated that those instructions equal about ten pages in the *Encyclopaedia Britannica.*[20]

And, reader, concerning the relation hereof to the previously mentioned cell-damaging mutations, the *New Encyclopedia Britannica* has the following to observe on all this. Listen:

> "In general, humans are among the most radiosensitive of all living organisms...The biologic effects of radiation in humans and other mammals are generally subdivided into (1) those that effect the body

of the exposed individual—somatic effects—and (2) those that affect the offspring of the exposed individual—genetic, or heritable, effects...

Every type of biologic effect of radiation, irrespective of its precise nature, results from injury to the cell, the microscopic building block of which all living organisms are composed...The effects of radiation on the cell include interference with cell division, damage to chromosomes, damage to genes, mutations...

Any type of molecule in the cell can be altered by irradiation, but the DNA of the genetic material is thought to be the cell's most critical target, since damage to a single gene may be sufficient to profoundly alter the cell...And those changes that remain unrepaired or misrepaired may give rise to permanent changes, mutations, in the affected genes or in the chromosomes on which the genes are carried

(more regressive "evolution", reader!)...

Gene damage, mutations, resulting from radiation-induced damage to DNA, have been produced experimentally in many types of organisms. And in general, the frequency of a given mutation increases in proportion to the dose of radiation...Even a small dose of radiation given to a large number of individuals, may introduce mutant genes into a population

("evolved" backward, reader!)...

By breaking both strands of the DNA molecule, radiation can also break the chromosome fibre and so interfere with cell division, thereby altering the structure and number of chromosomes in the cell. Chromosomal changes of this kind may alter its properties in various other ways. And chromosome breaks that fail to heal, may cause the loss of an essential part of the gene...When adjoining chromosome fibers in the same nucleus are broken, the broken ends may join together in such a way that the sequence of genes on the chromosomes is changed...

The tissues of the embryo, like others composed of rapidly proliferating cells, are highly radiation-sensitive...For example, when exposure occurs while an organ is forming, malformation of the organ may result. While exposure at a later stage is more likely to produce a functional abnormality. And a wide variety of radiation-induced malformations have been observed in experimentally irradiated rodents.[21]

Yes reader, and prior to rodents—as the writer saw visibly in Genetics college class—such malformations were profusely caused in scientific, genetical study of the much used fruit fly—*Drosophila melanogaster*. And the point that must be emphasized and needs to be noticed here, is that the resulting observation from all of these genetic experiments, was that the mutations always resulted in a regressive degrading of the subject experimented with.

And more recently, reader, scientific investigations have turned up the following confirming light.

A syndrome of abnormal traits appears in the hybrids ("the offspring produced by crossing two different species", dictionary) between certain strains of the fruit fly. The traits include partial sterility and greatly elevated rates of genetic mutations and chromosome rearrangements. Strains can be classified as paternally (P) contributing or maternally (M) contributing, so that only the hybrid sons and daughters of M females mated to P males show hybrid defective traits.

The hybrid defective genetic traits are caused by the action of a family of transposable genetic elements, that is, segments of the DNA genetic material, with the special (abnormal) ability to move from one chromosomal site to another...The cross of P males to M females activates the transposition mechanisms of these genetic elements, resulting often in mutations and chromosome rearrangements due to the chromosome breakage involved...

The ability of P factors to thus transpose has made them especially useful for manipulating DNA molecules (so, reader, regressive mutations can be "manipulated"—keep that significant point in mind!)...This effect of the P factor on the organism involved is the hybrid defective syndrome, which is highly detrimental...Thus the P factor and other transposable elements might make a positive contribution to the evolution of their hosts by additional mutations and chromosome rearrangements...And the reproductive incompatibility between P and M strains could, in some conditions, aid in the process of splitting one species into two...In that case, the resulting detrimental traits in some of the hybrids between the two subspecies would yield natural selection that would favor further reproductive isolation and perhaps eventual splitting into separate species.[22]

So, reader—herein we see Darwin's proposed and professed "natural selection" and consequent "survival of the fittest" new species rather accounted for by induced, manipulated mutation!—regressive "evolution" indeed!

And amid all of this above scientific background of the causes of mutations—here we have plain and simple, a present-day scientific admission to a more than likely explanation for the much touted evolution! Evolution said to occur, professedly, over long ages—but by the above shown to be such as could happen, and does, as experimentally manipulated and induced!

Yes, reader, plainly scientifically supportable and demonstrable means that today offer a very viable substitute alternative to replace Darwin's unproved evolutionary theory. So herein we see that in the race's constant decadence, rather than being an upbuilding matter of the "survival of the fittest", it's plainly a downgrading matter of the unhappy survival of the unfittest hybrid mutants!

This as stated in the following recent scientific admission, reader. Listen:

> "Dr. David Samuel, of Virginia Bioinformatics Institute, asserts that aging is caused largely by DNA mutations in cellular bodies called mitochondria, as new studies suggest. Vulnerability to DNA mutation restricts lifespans of most mammals to less than 100 years of age. This is a fundamental advance in continued research. Anything that reduces the ability of a species to resist DNA mutations could cut lifespans. That could include genetically modified (mutated) organisms.[23]

And, unfortunately for us homo sapiens, reader, as previously, this scientist pinpoints "mammals" as the most harmfully vulnerable species. And, scientist-geneticist Monroe Strickberger, in his monumental 868 page university-level book, *Genetics*, agreeingly applies as follows.

> Induced mutation rates seem to be much higher in mammals (due to)...the much longer generation time in mammals...And such an extreme sensitivity to induced mutation—perhaps caused by increased amounts of DNA—would be extremely disadvantageous to mammals...

> The longer generation time of mammals would permit them to accumulate gene and chromosome mutations much more readily...Radiation that produces a large number of ions (electricity) along a path, would be expected to have a greater chance of producing a mutation...(There is) a greater frequency of abnormalities for the larger chromosome species...

Ageing effects are also known, so that seed and pollen stored for long periods of time show increased mutation rates...Most of these observations support the idea that spontaneous mutations occur at a fairly constant rate and therefore accumulate with the passing of time.[24]

It all makes sense, reader—but how about his assertion about mutations being induced, or, manipulated as also previously suggested? Let us let this genetics expert illustratively explain as follows.

"Until 1927, an understanding of the causes of mutation as well as the accumulation of new mutations was greatly handicapped...until two factors were brought together: (1) sensitive detection methods, and (2) discovery and effective employment of mutation-producing agents, or mutagens.

Muller demonstrated the first artificial induction of mutations through measurement of the effect of large doses of x-rays on the mutation...Since then, high-energy radiation has proved to be one of the most effective mutagens, and it is used in numerous present-day studies.

Considering what radiation is, the visible light we observe is only a small part of the electromagnetic spectrum, which consists of energy in the form of a variety of wavelengths. As these wavelengths become shorter, the energy they contain becomes stronger and more penetrating. When x-rays were discovered, they were rapidly adapted for use in diagnostic medical procedures because of their penetrating abilities.

However, in the process of penetration, high-energy irradiation also produces ions ("a particle of matter bearing an electric charge", dictionary), by colliding with atoms and releasing electrons, which in turn collide with other atoms releasing further electrons, etc.

(resulting in damaging "free radicals", reader!)

> The change in electron number, transforms a stable atom or molecule into the reactive ionic state. Thus along the track of each high-energy ray, a train of ions is formed which can initiate a variety of chemical reactions. Such irradiation is called ionizing radiation. Measurement is in terms of an electrostatic unit of charge. Another unit, the rad, measures irradiation in terms of energy absorbed by material.

> Experiments with high-energy radiation showed soon after 1927 that induced mutation rates depend strongly upon radiation dosage, thus, the greater the dosage, the greater the mutation rate...According to this hypothesis, the high energy rays themselves or the ionizing (electrifying) particles produced, impinge as "hits" upon genes and chromosomes, each hit having a very high probability of causing a distinct mutation."[25]

And in previous context, reader, the *New Encyclopedia Britannica*, adds to such insight as follows.

> "The cause of mutations is usually some form of damage to the DNA or chromosomes that result in some change that can be seen...They may occur in either somatic (body) or germ (reproductive) cells. Mutations that occur in germ cells may be transmitted to subsequent generations"

—regressive "evolution" again, reader!

So—rather than the professed surviving "fittest" that are being passed on generation after generation in the race, it is as scientifically seen, indeed often surviving unfittest hybrid mutants that are being passed on! Little wonder the race of homo sapiens is continually waning and degrading from generation to generation!

And, reader, the oldest historical record on earth certainly certifies such. Listen: "Now it came to pass, when men began to multiply on the face of the earth...there were giants on the earth in those days" (Gen. 6:1, 4). And just how giant they were, reader, was shown to Ellen White as she records as follows first concerning man as created at the beginning, and then after being resurrected at the end.

Listen:

> God said to His Son, "Let us make man in our image." As Adam came forth from the hand of his Creator, he was of noble height and of beautiful symmetry. He was twice as tall as men now living upon the earth, and was well proportioned...Eve was not quite as tall as Adam. Her head reached a little above his shoulders. She, too, was noble, perfect in symmetry, and very beautiful.[26]

> The Son of God calls forth the sleeping saints...All come forth from their graves the same in stature as when they entered the tomb. Adam, who stands among the risen throng, is of lofty height and majestic form, in stature but little below the Son of God. He presents a marked contrast to the people of later generations; in this one respect is shown the great degeneracy of the race...Sin had defaced and almost obliterated the divine image; but...restored to the tree of life in the long-lost Eden, the redeemed will grow up to the full stature of the race in its primeval glory.[27]

Nice advance information, reader—but, here we still are in this murky and mutational slough of despond, not really knowing all the why's and wherefore's. And—we have company!—scientific company—who don't have all the answers as to the why's either. For small example, listen as they time and time again exhibit such lack as follows!

Two important questions we ask are: (1) What accounts for the high prevalence of these deleterious genes, and (2) What, if anything, can we do to get rid of them? The reasons for their high frequency are not yet fully agreed upon, although there is little question that they all arise originally through mutation...Thus if deleterious genes are not eliminated by selection, they will gradually increase in frequency in accord with their mutation rate.[28]

And:

Humans are among the most radiosensitive of all living organisms...Every type of biologic effect of radiation, irrespective of its precise nature, results from injury to the cell...The mechanisms through which these changes are produced are not yet fully understood, but each change is thought to be the end result of chemical alterations that are initiated by (induced?!) radiation as it randomly traverses the cell.[29]

And:

Infrared rays increased the efficiency of chromosomal aberrations, but some of these combined effects of infrared and x-rays are also time-dependent or temperature-sensitive. These effects as many others, are therefore associated with premutational and postmutational stages at which mutational resistance or repair can be distinctly modified. The mechanisms by which these interactions occur, however, are not known.[30]

And:

Mutations are induced by exposure to mutagens. Most mutagens cause specific chemical changes in the informational content of the DNA...Major changes in gene expression occur and are transmitted to progeny cells through changes in the signals that control genes that are transcribed into ribonucleic acid (RNA).The mechanisms by which differentiation is controlled are not known.[31]

So, admitted big scientific "blind spots", reader!—and how widespread are these mysteriously-caused aberrations? Listen:

> "Changes in the genes have obviously deleterious effects...Although not all birth defects are genetically produced, the proportion of genetically-caused defectives among them is undoubtedly high...The effect of deleterious genes must touch at least a majority of our population."[32]

That is regressively backward "evolution", reader!

And additionally, as follows—

> Similar considerations also apply to sublethal radiation effects, such as perturbations of growth rate, reproduction, and behavior. These responses to radiation stress have consequences for both the individual organism, and for the population, community, or ecosystem of which it is a part.[33]

So, reader—strangely a mystery to even the highly trained scientist element, is this regressive mutating degradation of actually the whole global population, now found to be actually, unfit hybrid mutants! Admittedly, a mysterious deleterious, debilitating mutating hugely beyond any way of explanation by natural means—as seen in the illustrating following.

Listen:

> "Mutagenic activity...has been shown to be affected by enzymes or catalases produced within the cell, so that if enzyme poisons are added, the mutation rate is increased...The need for such chemical explanations arises because of the relatively inadequate

amount of background radiation that would be sufficient to account for observed mutation rates in most organisms.

In Drosophila, for example, Muller calculated that the spontaneous mutation rate was about 1300 times larger than the rate expected on the basis of background irradiation."[34]

Astounding, reader, this largely unaccountable mutating! Causing one to ask, whatever, then, could be causing such a stupendously unusual amount of mutating in the population beyond that which would normally be expected?!

Unmasking the Mutating Masquerader

Well, reader, it's fortunate that, unlike the scientific community as above, we don't have to lie in limbo as to having the answer as to why there is so stupendously much unaccountable mutational effect in the global population. No, it was all long ago recorded "for our admonition", as to a causative malign, inducing manipulating going on behind the scenes! Listen: "Then to Adam He said, "Because you have heeded the voice of your wife, and have eaten from the tree of which I commanded you, saying, 'You shall not eat of it'", "Cursed is the ground for your sake; in toil you shall eat of it all the days of your life. Both thorns and thistles it shall bring forth to you" (Gen. 3:17, 18).

"Thorns and thistles", reader—simply descriptive, of course, of the huge, unending, and burgeoning array of such devilish annoyances that bedevil mankind the globe around!

Yes, "devilish", because obviously all such was and is the devil's work! Of God's work, on the other hand, it was inscribed: "Then God saw everything that He had made, and indeed, it was very good" (Gen. 1:31). So, the above-mentioned "curse" was the enemy's doing—not a good God's!

Yes, reader—"give the devil an inch, and he'll take a mile!"—and, he certainly did! And Christ Himself, in parabolic form, agreeingly showed such to be the very case in this matter. Listen as follows.

"When the grain had sprouted and produced a crop, then the tares (weeds) also appeared. So the servants of the owner came and said to him, 'Sir, did you not sow good seed in your field? How then does it have tares? He said to them, 'An enemy has done this'...He Who sows the good seed is the Son of Man. The field is the world and the good seeds are the sons of the kingdom, but the tares are the sons of the wicked one. The enemy who sowed them is the devil" (Matt. 13:26–28, 37–39).

And Ellen White was relatingly shown as follows, reader. Listen:

> "Christ never planted the seeds of death in the system. Satan planted these seeds when he tempted Adam to eat of the tree of knowledge, which meant disobedience to God.
>
> Not one noxious plant was placed in the Lord's great garden, but after Adam and Eve sinned, poisonous herbs sprang up. In the parable of the sower the question was asked the master, "Didst not thou sow good seed in thy field? From whence then hath it tares?"
>
> The master answered, "An enemy hath done this" (Matt. 13:27, 28). All tares are sown by the evil one. Every noxious herb is of his sowing, and by his ingenious methods of amalgamation he has corrupted the earth with his tares."[35]

Further:

> The God of nature is perpetually at work. His infinite power works unseen, but manifestations appear in the effects which the work produces. The same God Who guides the planets works in the fruit orchard and in the vegetable garden. He never made a thorn, a thistle, or a tare. These are Satan's work, the result of degeneration (mutation et al!).[36]

And again:

> Vital energy (electric power!) is imparted to the
> mind through the brain; therefore the brain should
> never be dulled by the use of narcotics or excited by
> the use of stimulants...From beginning to end, the
> crime of using tobacco, opium, and harsh drug
> medication, has its origin in perverted knowl-
> edge...They are using the poisonous productions that
> Satan himself has planted to take the place of the tree
> of life, whose leaves are for the healing of the nations.
> Men are dealing in liquors and narcotics that are
> destroying the human family.[37]

Yes, typically, reader, the great enemy does the
malign, diabolical producing, but as mentioned, he slyly
works through others. And, along with such as above,
what a "crop", as we have already seen as to his manipulating mutating means, the enemy has produced
mammal-wise as well!

Listen further as science asserts!

> In domesticated animals, where breeding records
> had long been kept, numerous instances had been
> recorded of novel (new!) types called "sports"
> suddenly appearing. Short-legged varieties of sheep
> and dogs, tailless cats, and similar inherited anoma-
> lies could occasionally be traced to their origin in
> single animals.

> DeVries called these large effects mutations, and
> gathered evidence for the high frequency of such
> mutations...When crossing over (cross-breeding)
> occurs between translocation heterozygotes (varied
> gene pairs), recombination may produce individuals
> strikingly different from their immediate parents.

> In essence, therefore, such individuals result from
> recombination between old genetic material,
> although the novelty of their appearance seems to
> indicate a completely new or mutant effect...Finally,

the concept of mutation was broadened to include the origin of hereditary effects, large and small, that could be traced to unique changes within the genetic material.[38]

"Evolution" again, reader—and putting two and two together, here from science itself, we see and have documentary admissions that really become evidence of the enemy mastermind's manipulating, mutating modus operandi! And Ellen White stresses on "mastermind", saying: "Satan has great advantages. He possessed the wonderful intellectual power of an angel, of which few form any just idea."

Yes, reader, obviously all above were his malign, manipulating means, given time. And Strickberger on page 546 agreeingly asserts: "Most of these observations support the idea that spontaneous mutations occur at a fairly constant rate and therefore accumulate with time".

And there is no doubt, reader, that this mastermind does "make the most of the time" and opportunity! Let's hear it again:

"Induced (guess who is doing the inducing!) mutation rates seem to be much higher in mammals (due to)...the much longer generation time in mammals...

And such an extreme sensitivity to induced mutation—perhaps caused by increased amounts of DNA—would be extremely disadvantageous to mammals...Radiation that produces a large number of ions (electrical power!) along a path, would be expected to have a greater chance of producing a mutation...and abnormalities."

And speaking of electricity, reader, you have noticed over and over the profuse use of the term "power" all through. And the underlying meaning of the word nowadays is plain to all. For example, when my retirement home was ready, wiring and all, the electrician "turned on the power"—the electricity.

And just here, reader, taking his high points, author Noorbergen applies as follows in his chapter: "Electricity—the Vital Force." "No one single discovery has affected our civilization as much as that of electricity. But it was not until 1929 that the German psychiatrist Hans Berger personally involved every one of us by announcing that we are all individual electrical generators!

And in 1934, Dr. Charles Mayo of the famed Mayo Clinic supported Dr. Berger asserting that "minute electrical charges are vital to the functioning of the brain." And Ernst Weber, president of the Polytechnic Institute of New York, backed this, saying: "These wonderful waves exist in the human body, and are the vital force of the heart and nerves."

Early on Ellen White had recognized the value of electrical power. And not only was she foremost in advocating that electrical power was responsible for the operation of the human body, but she also even credited (as recently substantiated) electricity with providing the needed stimuli for the growth process in plantlife.

As far back as 1869 Ellen White said:

> "The brain nerves which communicate with the entire system are the only medium through which heaven can communicate with man and affect his inmost life. Whatever disturbs the circulation of the electric currents in the nervous system lessens the strength of the vital powers."

Further, in 1872:

God endowed man with so great a vital force that he has withstood the accumulation of disease brought upon the race as a consequence of perverted habits, and has continued for six thousand years. This fact of itself is evidence to us of the strength and electrical energy that God gave to man at the Creation.

All work being done in this rapidly expanding field of investigation indicates that electricity forms the basis for all of life's actions and experiences. *Electronics World* of April 1970, said it is:

A unique communications grid that binds all life together. Its phenomenon apparently works on a multi-input basis which operates beyond known physical laws.[39]

Well plain enough, then, reader, that the great enemy of God and man—the negative power who "operates beyond known physical laws", mysteriously to the scientific world—is the culprit who from behind the scenes is "inputting" and "inducing" and "manipulating" his diabolical and debilitating electrical "power" mutatingly in all creation!

Indeed, recall Ellen White's revealed assertion that, to this malign end, "Satan...has studied the secrets of the laboratories of nature, and he uses all of his power to control...in every place and in a thousand forms, Satan is exercising his power."

And in asserting that this mastermind fallen angel still has such power, reader, Ellen White has backing—that of the Word of God itself. As follows, listen!: "Jesus said to them, "I beheld Satan as lightning fall from heaven" (Luke 10:18, KJV)—and that is power, reader!—lightning being the most formidable manifestation of electrical power to us on earth.

The same power Christ had to contend with when the enemy tried to defeat and make Him sin at His wilderness trial. Listen: "Then Jesus was led up by the Spirit into the wilderness to be tempted (tested) by the devil...Then the devil took Him up into the holy city and set Him on the pinnacle of the temple...Again, the devil took Him up on an exceeding high mountain, and showed Him all the kingdoms of the world and their glory. And he said to Him, "All these things I will give You if You will fall down and worship me" (Matt. 4:5, 8, 9).

And on this audacious show of Satan's power, reader, Ellen White applies as follows.

> Fallen man is Satan's lawful captive...Satan will go to the length of his power to harass...He who dared to face and tempt and taunt our Lord, and who had power to take Him in his arms and carry Him to a pinnacle of the temple, and then up into an exceeding high mountain, will exercise his power to a great degree upon the present generation, who are almost wholly ignorant of Satan's subtlety and strength. In an astonishing manner he will affect the bodies of those...[40]

And on this significant matter of Satan working on our bodies with his malign, mutating electrical power, reader, she adds elsewhere as follows.

> The prince of darkness' agents...mediums...still claim to cure disease. They attribute their power to electricity, magnetism, or the so-called sympathetic remedies. In truth, they are but channels for Satan's electric currents. By this means he casts his spell over the bodies and the minds of men.[41]

And well does the writer, reader, recall personally and "shockingly" experiencing first-hand as above—as have many others too in working against the enemy in the Lord's work—concerning which volumes could be written! But, actually, my experience in such was second-hand, for indeed the enemy does work through others, the better to conceal and push his diabolical work.

The occasion was that I was assisting in an evangelistic series. Later in the series, after a meeting, those involved each later paid a visit to attendees whose names were assigned to them. So, next day I visited a family in a large city, and was courteously invited in. Then we sat around the table with our bibles, and proceeded to discuss things presented in the meetings.

But as the discussion continued, I noticed that there was a steady attempt to downgrade my observations. And then later on, the woman of the family excused herself and went aside into the sitting room. Out of the corner of my eye, I could see she was holding a large towel, with her eyes closed apparently praying.

Suddenly she arose and came toward me while holding this spread out towel out ahead of her—I somehow feeling as though a pressuring wave of power was enclosing me. Then, as she arrived right before me, she suddenly flipped up the towel to me, yelling "Take hold of it!" This power of suggestion came so forcefully, that I just automatically did so—much to my chagrin!

At that moment of contact, there was a great sound such as of a large electrical discharge, at which I became momentarily stupefied. Shortly gaining somewhat my senses and composure, as they looked on disdainfully, I grabbed my coat and hat and slipped out the door.

All the while feeling as if half drugged, reader, I finally arrived for our after-visiting meeting where we were to report on our visits. As I somewhat excitedly told of my misadventure, I asked them to pray over me to help release me from my stupor, the group looking on somewhat skeptically.

However, they dutifully did pray over me for the Lord's deliverance, which did bring some relief from the stupor. But, it was not until such was done again in our morning meeting that full relief providentially came.

And, it was only somewhat later, reader, that I realized what I had experienced when I somehow found that this family were spiritists, the woman being head of the spiritualist society for all that district. Then it was that I realized she had been praying to the devil for power to inflict me with.

And, reader, God's Word indeed reminds, that this "prince of the power of the air" operates "according to the working of Satan, with all power, signs, and lying wonders" (Eph. 2:2; 2 Thes. 2:9). Little wonder that the apostle Paul also warns: "We do not wrestle against flesh and blood, but against principalities, against powers, against the rulers of the darkness of this age, against spiritual hosts of wickedness" (Eph. 6:12).

And one of the many, but most significant, of those with both minds and bodies affected and afflicted by Satan's malevolent power, reader, Ellen White pinpoints warningly as follows.

> The encounter with the demoniacs of Gergesa had a lesson for the disciples. For, it showed the depths of degradation to which Satan is seeking to drag the whole human race...Satan's influence is constantly exerted upon men to distract the senses, control the mind for evil...He weakens the body, darkens the intellect, and debases the soul.[42]

So again, reader, we see Satan's target is also the body—as again as she shares as follows.

> I was informed that the inhabitants of earth had been degenerating, losing their strength and comeliness. Satan has the power of disease and death, and with every age the effects of the curse have been more visible, and the power of Satan more plainly seen…Every succeeding generation have been growing weaker and more subject to disease, and their life has been of shorter duration. Satan has been learning how to annoy and enfeeble the race.[43]

Christ, Who encountered many such in His day, reader, pinpoints such as follows. Listen:

> And behold, there was a woman who had a spirit of infirmity eighteen years, and was bent over and could in no way raise herself up. But when Jesus saw her, He called her to Him and said…"ought not this woman, being a daughter of Abraham, whom Satan has bound, be loosed from this bond?" (Luke 13:11–16).

Hence the needed warning, reader:

> None are in greater danger…than those who, notwithstanding the direct and ample testimonies of the Scriptures, deny the existence and agency of the devil and his angels…for they can distract our minds and disorder and torment our bodies.[44]

Warn she well might, reader, for she adds:

> The present enfeebled condition of the human family was presented before me. Every generation has been growing weaker and weaker, and disease of every form afflicts the race. Thousands of poor mortals with deformed, sickly bodies, shattered nerves, and gloomy minds are dragging out a miserable existence. Satan's power upon the human family increases. If the Lord should not soon come and destroy his power, the earth would erelong be depopulated.[45]

And in like vein, reader, elsewhere she adds:

> This fact of itself is enough evidence to us of the strength and electrical energy that God gave to man at his creation...If Adam, at his creation, had not been endowed with twenty times as much vital force as men now have, the race, with their present habits of living in violation of natural law, would have become extinct.[46]

So, reader—in view of all such Satan's uninhibited, behind the scenes electrically-induced mutating going on apace, degenerating generation after generation, little wonder that today, rather than being evolving into the fittest, we rather are increasingly unfittest hybrid mutants!

And speaking of "hybrid", reader—that too enters the devil's fauna-flora biologic attack picture as well. For, be sure with all his time spent scrutinizing "the laboratories of nature", he who figured out and utilized crossbreeding, doesn't come short in hybridizing either. And on this the dictionary explains: "To cross breed; produce from the union of two different species."

Now Ellen White, reader, used a similar term—amalgamate. And on this the dictionary says: "mating; to mix together; join; merge; coalesce." And with this meaning, from the light given her, she advises as follows.

> If there was one sin above another which called for the destruction of the race by the flood, it was the base crime of amalgamation of man and beast which defaced the image of God, and caused confusion everywhere. God purposed to destroy by a flood that powerful, long-lived race that had corrupted their ways before Him...
>
> Every species of animal which God had created were preserved in the ark. The confused species which

> God did not create (obviously dinosaurs and such prehistoric creatures), which were the result of amalgamation, were destroyed by the flood.[47]

And that such hybridizing amalgamation did occur, reader, can be seen in the trite but significant scriptural assertion as follows. Listen: "The earth also was corrupt before God, and the earth was filled with violence...for all flesh had corrupted their way on the earth" (Gen. 6:11, 12).

And also, reader, the fact that all of the dinosaur and such remains are found covered by enveloping soil or rock, fits this flood-destroyed-and-buried scenario to a "t"! Why proof is seen in that mastodons have been unearthed in the far north—which obviously was semi-tropical before the epoch-changing flood—with fresh grass still in their mouth, obviously as they were suddenly inundated. And on that point—such utterly massive amounts of mixed-up and mangled bones of these prehistoric creatures have been unearthed when excavating up north, that nothing but the biblical Flood could account for all such!

And if it seems somewhat far-fetched, reader, to suppose that by amalgamation-hybridization Satan had so perverted life-forms on the earth, let us realize that even before the flood, he had 1,500 years to bend his mastermind to studying to this malign end in "the laboratories of nature".

And further—though Satan cannot create—still, he can, and obviously has and does synchronize the elements of earth into devil-designed fabrications of his pestilent purposes. For, convincingly, science has by study and trial and error found that such "creating" out of what was created is possible. Listen as *The New Encyclopedia Britannica* previously quoted, under the article "light", in small part enlightens hereon as follows.

> Such manifestations are intimately linked with the studies of the properties of submicroscopic particles on the one hand and with the properties of the entire universe on the other. The creation of electromagnetic radiation from matter, and the creation of matter from radiation, both of which have been achieved, provide a fascinating insight.

So, reader, in this age of scientific cloning—and who knows what next!—with his masterful insight and understanding, we won't want to sell the devil short—short of "creating" to the extent he is able—even to that of the dinosaurs and all! And that we have away-out similar scientific scenarios coming on apace today, reader, following on in monkeying with that created, listen as researcher Denyse O'Leary in *Faith and Science* glaringly illustrates!

> Recently the *Washington Post* revealed that it has become routine to implant human cells in animals, for various purposes ("Of Mice, Men, and In-between" by Rick Weiss, November 20, 2004). These hybrid animals are called chimeras. They are created by placing human stem cells in animal fetuses.
>
> The National Academy of Sciences is trying to figure out how much human stuff can be put in an animal before it comes to be regarded as human. One proposal is to take stem cells harvested from embryos left over at fertility clinics and transfer them into an animal embryo.
>
> The "humanized" animals, Weiss explains, would be very useful for testing drugs and poisons. Others, such as Irving Weissman of Stanford, want to add human brain cells to animal brains, perhaps creating a mouse with a brain that is 100 per cent human. A recent article in *Trends in Biotechnology* (November

2004) provides a much more sober assessment than what you hear from the people who play lethal games with human embryos. Meanwhile, California is setting up a $3 billion dollar fund to enable experiments with human embryos (Los Angeles Times, November 22, 2004), and luring to the state the many who are willing to do them. This includes "therapeutic" cloning, which means creating embryos for research.[48]

So, reader, as said, let's not sell short super-smart Satan, who long ago studied into "the laboratories of nature". But, perhaps he learned the big ploys by previously experimenting on the more minor ones—like bears and lions, say. For, surely, with all the scenario background we have seen, we wouldn't for a moment suppose that God made bears and lions—that is, not like the cruel, carnivorous bears and lions as we know them today!

No, no, reader—not for a moment did a kind and loving God create anything that was unkind and cruel and bloodthirsty and unloving and unlike Himself. As we saw, He was able to say of all He created that it all was "very good." And thus as shown to His servant Ellen White, let us notice as follows.

After the earth with its teeming animal and vegetable life had been called into existence, man, the crowning work of the Creator, the one for whom the beautiful earth had been fitted up, was brought upon the stage of action...

After the creation of Adam, every living creature ("kind") was brought before him to receive its name; he saw that to each had been given a companion...And the Lord God planted a garden eastward in Eden; and there He put the man whom He had formed. Everything that God had made was the perfection of beauty.

While they remained true to God, Adam and his companion were to bear rule over all the earth. Unlimited control was given them over every living thing. The lion and the lamb sported peacefully around them, or lay down together at their feet. The happy birds flitted about them without fear...

With every living creature, from the mighty leviathan that plays among the waters, to the insect mote that floats in the sunbeam, Adam was familiar. He had given to each its name, and he was acquainted with the nature and habits of all...The order and harmony of creation spoke to them of infinite wisdom and power.[49]

Again:

Adam was surrounded with everything his heart could wish. Every want was supplied. There was no sin, and no signs of decay in glorious Eden...The happy songsters caroled forth their free, joyous songs of praise to their Creator. The peaceful beasts in happy innocence played about Adam and Eve, obedient to their word.[50]

And further:

Very happy were the holy pair in Eden. Unlimited control was given them over every living thing. The lion and the lamb sported peacefully and harmlessly around them, or slumbered at their feet. Birds of every variety of color and plumage flitted among the trees and flowers and about Adam and Eve, while their mellow-toned music echoed among the trees in sweet accord to their praises of their Creator.[51]

And added to this, reader, in her book *The Ministry of Healing*, page 261, she wrote:

"In the Garden that God prepared as a home for His children...On the branches, the birds caroled their songs of praise. Under their shadow the creatures of the earth sported together without fear." And the reason they had no fear, she shows on page 396 of *Counsels On Diet and Foods*, where a trite statement says: "God gave to Adam charge of the garden, to dress it, and to care for it, saying, "To you it shall be for meat" (old English for food). "One animal was not to destroy another animal for food."

And why not, reader?—simply because in their perfection, it wasn't their nature to. Obviously, bestiality, of both creature and man, is the product of sin and its malign consequences, of Satan and his mutatingly beastly degenerative work. And, reader, God has left on Record, the proof positive of just that. That is, the nature of man and creature in the Word-promised earth made new, is identical to that of the edenic life. Listen as "the gospel prophet" describes as follows. "They shall not hurt nor destroy in all My holy mountain, says the Lord...The wolf and the lamb shall feed together, and (note!) the lion shall eat straw like the ox" (Isa. 65:25). This is simply their getting back to their original, God-given diet, reader, as shown by the following. Listen: "Also, to every beast of the earth, to every bird of the air, and to everything that creeps on the earth, I have given every green herb for food" (Gen. 1:30).

Further inspired glimpses: "The desert shall rejoice and blossom as the rose...for waters shall burst forth in the wilderness, and streams in the desert...no lion shall be there (as we now know them), nor shall any ravenous beast, for, it shall not be found there" (Isa. 35:1–9).

And the confirmation, reader, of the former assertion that the lion as we now know them as indeed ravenous beasts will not be there, we see in the prophet's further portrayal as follows. "The wolf also shall dwell with the lamb, the leopard shall lie down with the young goat, the calf and the young lion and the fatling together; and a little child shall lead them. The cow and the bear shall graze (grass!), and the young ones shall lie down together. And the lion shall eat straw like the ox (a vegetarian, reader!). The nursing child shall play by the cobra's hole, and the weaned child shall put his hand in the viper's den. They shall not hurt nor destroy in all My holy mountain says the Lord" (Isa.11:6–9).

And the reason, again, reader, that they don't destroy?—simply because both their nature and their physical makeup, all mutated nature gone, are once again edenic. And we see the proof positive in the bear and lion "grazing" and "eating straw or hay!" Can you see the present the lion, with its pointed teeth, subsisting on such an otherworldly diet?! For note—then and there it doesn't just pick a few sprigs of grass—it eats hay like the ox—which to live consumes hay by the bale!

No, reader—There, the bears and lions will be, as in the beginning, just big playful teddy-bears and pussycats! Listen as follows, to inspiration, as Ellen White describes that shown her of the life in the earth made new.

> I saw another field full of all kinds of flowers, and as I plucked them, I cried out, "They will never fade!" ...Then we entered a field full of all kinds of beasts—the lion, the lamb, the leopard, the wolf, all together in perfect union. We passed through the midst of them, and they followed on peacefully after. Then we entered a woods.... and (quoting Ezekiel 34:25) we all cried out, 'We will dwell safely in the wilderness and sleep in the woods.[52]

As she had said, reader, there is no fear there, for, neither, thankfully, is there any sin or Satan, and so no diabolically mutated perversion such as we suffer so from today. So surely we will want above all to be there!

And praise and thank our good God that He has made it fully possible for us to be there—and, as we have been seeing, has written it all down for us in "black and white" in His Word past and present.

And that given Ellen White, reader, fully encourages that There we can and will indeed be fully free from Satan's mutating and sin-causing power. Listen as such is encouragingly promised as follows.

> The Plan of Redemption contemplates our complete recovery from the power of Satan. Christ always separates the contrite soul from sin. He came to destroy the work of the devil, and He has made provision that the Holy Spirit shall be imparted to every repentant soul, to keep him or her from sinning...So a holy temper, a Christ-like life, is accessible to every repenting, believing child of God.[53]

And that this God-given "plan of redemption" deliverance is accessible and occurring right now for all who will, reader, listen as follows.

> Satan knows that only through their transgression of God's law can he obtain power over them. His accusations against them arise solely from his enmity to Christ. Through the Plan of Salvation, Jesus is breaking Satan's hold upon the human family, and rescuing souls from his power...Satan has no power to pluck them out of the hand of the Savior. Not one soul who in penitence and faith has claimed His protection, will Christ permit to pass under the enemy's power.[54]

Indeed gospel "good news", reader!—and as you noticed, detailed in God's great "plan of redemption and salvation." And so shall we not fervently praise and thank our good God for revealing to us these great delivering and saving plans? Listen as the servant of the Lord further extols its saving virtues as follows.

The central theme of the Bible, the theme about which every other in the whole book clusters, is the redemption plan, the restoration in the human soul of the image of God. From the first intimation of hope, in the sentence pronounced in Eden, to that last glorious promise of the Revelation, "They shall see His face, and His name shall be in their foreheads," the theme and burden of every book and every passage of the Bible is the unfolding of this wondrous theme—man's uplifting by the power of God.[55]

And how thankful we "heirs of salvation" can be, reader, that God's saving and delivering power is infinitely greater than that of the enemy! The apostle John put it: "You are of God, little children, and have overcome them, because He Who is in you is greater than he who is in the world (worldlings)" (1 John 4:4). And how blessed, reader, that our God of love has graciously given us this saving redemption plan in plain language, so as to be fully obtainable and understandable to us all, young and old.

And yet, reader, tragically, unbelievably almost in face of all this, the apostle John also here asserts that: "The whole world lies in wickedness!" (1 John 5:19). How ever could this be when the great God of love—even after we had turned our backs on Him in sin—"so loved the world that He gave His only begotten Son, (as a human, to cruelly die so we could be forgiven and saved!) that whoever believes in Him should not perish, but have everlasting life?" (John 3:16).

Again—how could practically "the whole world", in face of all this, have turned wickedly away? Well, reader, the apostle doesn't leave us in a quandary wondering as to the answer. For, a few pages further on in the Word, he opens up to our view the astounding answer. Listen as graphically follows.

"Now a great sign appeared in heaven: a woman...being with Child, she cried out in labor and in pain to give birth. And another sign appeared in heaven: behold, a great, fiery red dragon...His tail drew a third of the stars (angels in prophecy) of heaven and threw them to the earth. And the dragon stood before the woman who was ready to give birth, to devour her Child as soon as it was born. She bore a male Child Who was to rule all nations with a rod of iron. And her Child was caught up to God and His throne.

And war broke out in heaven: Michael (Christ's name as heavenly Commander) and His angels fought with the dragon; and the dragon and his angels fought, but they did not prevail, nor was a place found for them in heaven any longer. So the great dragon was cast out, that serpent of old, called the Devil and Satan, who deceives the whole world; he was cast to the earth, and his angels were cast out with him...

Therefore rejoice, O heavens, and you who dwell in them! But woe to the inhabitants of the earth and the sea! For the devil has come down to you, having great wrath, because he knows that he has a short time...And the dragon was enraged with the woman (the church in prophecy), and he went to make war with the rest of her offspring, who keep the commandments of God and have the testimony of Jesus Christ...the testimony of Jesus is the spirit of prophecy" (the Spirit giving the gift of prophecy) (Rev. 12:1–17; 19:10).

So, reader, here again we plainly see that though Satan cannot successfully fight against God Himself, he does so by attacking His commandments and law and those who keep them. For, therein God's very will is verbally expressed, such being the very basis of His universal government itself. And it is in this deceptively underhanded way, wherein he brainwashes souls into feeling that that good "law of liberty" as the Word rightly calls it, rather restricts their liberty, that the devil has been able to "deceive the whole world" and win them over to his side!

And thus, also, reader, was exactly how Lucifer-Satan did with the heavenly angels, and then following, with hoodwinked Eve and Adam in Eden. So the prophet Ezekiel uses a despot-antagonist of God's people of old to aptly symbolize Lucifer-Satan and these his crooked brainwashing past activities. And that Bible commentators thus apply this to Lucifer-Satan, reader, is illustrated in the following by Billy Graham.

Listen:

> "Ezekiel 28 sets forth the typology of Satan...an earthly prince of the city of Tyre...seems to be an earthly symbol of Satan...an earthly illustration of the heavenly Lucifer who became the devil." (*Angels: God's Secret Agents*, page 80).

So the prophet applies, reader: "The word of the Lord came to me again, saying, "Son of man, say to the prince of Tyre, 'Thus says the Lord God:..."your heart is lifted up, and you say, 'I am a god, I sit in the seat of gods, in the midst of the seas (multitudes, in prophecy),' yet you are a man, and not a god, though you set your heart as the heart of a god.

"Behold, you are wiser than Daniel! There is no secret that can be hidden from you! (even in "the laboratories of nature", recall!). With your wisdom and your understanding you have gained riches for yourself...and your heart is lifted up because of your riches...You were the seal of perfection, full of wisdom and perfect in beauty.

You were in Eden, the garden of God (Lucifer-Satan was the only being ever there beside Adam and Eve)...You were the anointed cherub who covers; I established you so; you were on the holy mountain of God...you were perfect in your ways from the day you were created until iniquity was found in you...you became filled with violence within, and you sinned...you defiled your sanctuaries by the multitude of your iniquities" (Eze. 28:1–18).

How all "stranger than fiction", reader—and yet, as divinely revealed, how unevadebly plain that Lucifer-Satan had thus "sinned!" In actuality, God the great Judge, is here arraining Lucifer-Satan into court as the accused, with the legal accusation being that he had "sinned" in breaking God's Law.

This being the case, reader, in this momentous and vital case, it needs to be seen as to just what sin is and what it means before God and His law to engage in sin. And, of course, since a just God uses that legal term in His Word, it is only logical and certain that His Word will plainly give the needed answer.

So, reader, listen as that Word does plainly give the answer as follows: "Whosoever committeth sin transgesseth also the law, for sin is the transgression of the Law" (1 John 3:4, KJV); and: "Whoever commits sin also commits lawlessness, and sin is lawlessness" (NKJV); and: "Everyone who sins breaks the law; in fact, sin is lawlessness" (NIV). So plainly and unequivocably, reader—sin is the breaking of God's holy law, thus making one lawless. And the apostle Paul plainly applies this enlightenment, saying as follows.

"Now we know that whatever the law says, it says to those who are under the law (jurisdiction of), that every mouth may be stopped, and all the world may become guilty (of breaking it) before God...for by the law is the knowledge of sin"...What shall we say then? Is the law sin? Certainly not! On the contrary, I would not have known sin except through the law...Therefore the law is holy, and the commandment holy and just and good" (Rom. 3:19, 20; 7:7, 12).

Why our good God, reader, in giving us His good law, had only our own good in mind and at heart. As He plainly emphasizes this, as follows, listen. "Oh, that they had such a heart in them that they would fear (reverence) Me, and always keep all My commandments, that it might be well with them and with their children forever...You shall walk in all the ways which the Lord your God has commanded you, that you may live and that it may be well with you, and that you may prolong your days...And these words which I command you today shall be in your heart" (Deut. 5:29–33; 6:5, 6).

Doesn't that all just make sense, reader? When teenagers, for instance, now heady with the desire to have their own supposedly good way, kick the good traces put about them by wiser and kindly parents—what harm invariably results later on much to their sad chagrin?! Ask, for further rexample—is it law-keepers, or, law-breakers, who infest our correctional centers and jails?

No, reader, a wiser and good God well knew that the restraint of law, God's law, and man's—since He had given us free-will and freedom of choice—was an absolute necessity. Recently, a not-so-welcome parking ticket drove home this fact as it stated: "At times traffic laws inconvenience individuals, but in such cases it should be remembered that these laws are for the general good, and the individual charged should willingly comply in the interest of the public."

Reader—how could one find fault with that just and reasonable reminder? No—it reminds of a school teacher's teaching notes I came across once. Listen:

God gave us laws to show us the way to happiness. They explain to us the best way to live to this end, and protect us from doing those things which hurt and destroy us. But when people ignore God's laws, to mention a few, things like that listed as follows happens to them.

Consequent dishonesty and theft bring dishonor, while other results can be drunkenness, licentiousness, disease, suffering and misery, disaster and immature death. But when people obey God's laws, there result freedom from harm and shame, blessings of all types such as truly real freedom from disease, and premature death, with rewarding real lasting happiness and prosperity, rounded out with a long and enjoyable life—and the prospect of eternal life in the end.

Again, reader, in face of all such, can we not plainly see why our good and loving God gave us—His whole Universe—these good and protecting laws? Can we not also see, then, why its necessity and universality are plainly indicated in His good Guide-book given for our guidance and protection and blessing?

And showing the universality thereof, reader, listen as the following "written for our admonition" plainly reveals such. "O Lord, You alone are the Lord; You made heaven, the heaven of heavens, with all their host...the host of heaven worships You" (Neh. 9:6). And: "The Lord has established His throne in heaven, and His kingdom rules over all. Bless the Lord you His angels, who excel in strength, who do His word, heeding the voice of His word. Bless the Lord, all you His hosts, you ministers of His, who do His pleasure. Bless the Lord, all His works, in all places of His dominion" (Psalm 103:17–22).

And Christ Himself inferred this universality, reader, teaching us to pray: "Our Father in heaven, hallowed be Your name. Your kingdom come. Your will be done on earth as it is in heaven" (Matt. 6:10). And note how as follows His prophet Daniel foretells this blessed event and day. "Then the kingdom and dominion under the whole heaven, shall be given to the saints of the Most High. His kingdom is an everlasting kingdom, and all dominions shall serve and obey Him" (Dan. 7:27).

And on the very last page of His holy Word, reader, God has His prophet John the beloved picture that great day when His obedient saints are thus rewarded. Listen: "Behold, I am coming quickly, and My reward is with Me, to give everyone according to his work...Blessed are those who do His commandments, that they may have the right to the tree of life, and may enter through the gates into the city" (Rev. 22:12, 14).

The Created Attacks Its Creator!

So it is more than plain, reader, that Lucifer-Satan was totally wrong—unlike the universal host, who obey God—in casting off the good restraints of God's holy law, thus becoming, as pointed out, lawless and so sinful, thus really making an audacious attack upon God and His universal government. Notice how John the beloved makes this more than plain, saying: "Whoever commits sin also commits lawlessness...for the devil has sinned from the beginning" (1 John 3:4, 8).

And Christ Himself, reader, certifies this, saying as follows to those who were planning to crucify Him. "You are of your father the devil, and the desires of your father you want to do. He was a murderer (breaking of the 6th commandment) from the beginning, and does not stand in the truth, because there is no truth in him...for he is a liar (breaking of the 9th commandment) and the father of it" (John 8:44). Again, reader, plainly revealing Lucifer-Satan to be the source of sin.

But, how more sad yet, that Lucifer-Satan was able to, through the Fall, introduce sin right into this edenically pure and perfect world. Worse yet, to further by this fact, become "the prince" or ruler of the world in place of fallen Adam and Eve. And worse even yet, to them in their fallen and sin-loving condition, now be able to cause them and their progeny to hear and follow his voice and dictates, rather than rightfully, God's.

Reader—in view of this tragic and sin-enslaving scenario and situation—what ever could, would, a sin-hating God, unable now to manifest Himself to fallen sinners—yet still longing to somehow yet save them—be able to do to somehow yet reveal this and His plan of redeeming salvation to them?

Well, that great Plan, divinely formulated "ere we knew Him", already had a simple yet sagacious formula prepared to solve this sad exigency. A solution, the results of which, we have already been using from the beginning of these studies—and that is simply God's will revealed to us through His holy Word, the Bible. That Word received from God and relayed to us through chosen prophet-servants, His secret agents, as it were, here on earth.

The apostle Peter describes it thus: "And so we have the prophetic word confirmed, which you do well to heed, as a light that shines in a dark place…knowing this first, that no prophecy of Scripture is of any private interpretation, for prophecy never came by the will of man, but holy men of God spoke as they were moved by the Holy Spirit" (2 Pet. 1:19–21).

And thank our good God, reader, that there were, among the sin-loving inhabitants of earth, sin-hating, God-fearing and obedient servants of His whom He could thus use. Men whom like Enoch of whom it could be said that he "walked with God", and Moses, the "servant, and friend of God." And so it was that all down through time, God by His Spirit spoke to these obedient prophets the Word He asked them to speak on His behalf to the people.

For trite example: "The words of Jeremiah the son of Hilkiah, of the priests…the word of the Lord came to me, saying: "Before I formed you in the womb…I ordained you a prophet to the nations…For you shall go to all to whom I send you, and whatever I command you, you shall speak. Do not be afraid of their faces, for I am with you to deliver you...Behold, I have put My words in your mouth" (Jer. 1:1–9).

And a further insight into the mechanics hereof, reader, is that of the apostle John, saying as follows. "The revelation of Jesus Christ, which God gave Him to show His servants...and He sent and signified it by His angel to His servant John, who bore witness to the word of God, and to the testimony of Jesus Christ, to all things that he saw. Blessed is he who reads and those who hear the words of this prophecy, and keep those things which are written in it...He who has an ear, let him hear what the Spirit says" (Rev. 1:1–3; 2:7).

Makes sense, doesn't it, reader, that when God goes to all that trouble to send His Word to us for our edification and guidance and so salvation, that He would expect us to "hear" or pay attention to what His Spirit says thus to us. And thus it was that Christ instructed as follows: "It is to your advantage that I go away, for...if I depart, I will send Him (the Holy Spirit) to you. And when He has come, He will convict the world of sin, and of righteousness, and of judgement...when He, the Spirit of truth, has come, He will guide you into all truth, for...whatever He hears He will speak" (John 16:7–13).

Thus it was, reader, that Spirit-led Paul in turn wrote: "I, brethren, when I came to you...my speech and my preaching were not with persuasive words of human wisdom, but in demonstration of the Spirit and of power, that your faith should not be in the wisdom of men, but in the power of God...God has revealed them to us through His Spirit. For the Spirit searches all things, yes, the deep things of God...These things we also speak...which the Holy Spirit teaches, comparing spiritual things with spiritual" (1 Cor. 2:1–13).

And the apostle, reader, follows such up declaring the purpose of his Spirit-indited preaching of the Word, saying as follows. "For whatever things were written before were written for our learning, that we through the patience and comfort of the Scriptures might have hope…Now may the God of hope fill you with all joy and peace in believing, that you may abound in hope by the power of the Holy Spirit…that I might be a minister of Jesus Christ to the Gentiles, ministering the gospel of God, that the offering of the Gentiles might be acceptable, sanctified by the Holy Spirit…in word and in deed to make the Gentiles obedient…

The grace of our Lord Jesus Christ be with you all…Who is able to establish you according to my gospel and the preaching of Jesus Christ, according to the revelation (revealing) of the mystery kept secret since the world began but now has been made manifest, and by the prophetic Scriptures has been made known to all nations, according to the commandment of the everlasting God, for obedience to the faith" (Rom. 15:4, 13–18; 16:20–26).

Again, reader, the bottom line—"for obedience" to God and His law—thus putting up that guarding fence around us to keep and spare us from evil and all its trials and troubles and eventual death. Just as the good Lord has counselled from of old: "My son, if you receive My words, and treasure My commands within you, so that you incline your ear to wisdom, and apply your heart to understanding…He stores up sound wisdom for the upright; He is a shield to those who walk uprightly; He guards the paths of the just, and preserves the way of His saints…

My son, do not forget My law, but let your heart keep My commands; for length of days and long life and peace they will add to you…my son, let them not depart from your eyes; keep sound wisdom and discretion, so they will be life to your soul and grace to your neck. Then you will walk safely in your way...For the Lord will be your confidence...the wise shall inherit glory" (Prov. 2:1–8; 3:1, 2, 21–26, 35).

So seeing that rewarding obedience with every good gift ending with eternal life is our loving Lord's supreme motive, reader, what would naturally be our attitude to Him and His Word and law of love? Listen as Job, tested therein as few others responds: "He knows the way that I take—when He has tested me, I shall come forth as gold. My foot has held fast to His steps; I have kept His way and not turned aside. I have not departed from the commandment of His lips; I have treasured the words of His mouth more than my necessary food" (Job 23:10–12).

And the prophet Jeremiah, reader, also tested long by persecution almost to despair was still able to testify as follows. Listen: "Woe is me, my mother, that you have borne me, a man of strife and a man of contention to the whole earth...every one of them curses me!...O Lord, You know; remember me and visit me, and...in Your enduring patience, do not take me away. Know that for Your sake I have suffered rebuke. Your words were found, and I ate them, and Your Word was to me the joy and rejoicing of me heart" (Jer. 15:10, 15, 16).

And our Savior, reader, also when tested certainly as none other, as after forty days of fasting the devil urged Him to use His Own power to save Himself by turning stones into bread, still was able to assert: "Man shall not live by bread alone, but by every word that proceeds from the mouth of God" (Matt. 4:4). The acid test, reader, of the truth of these assertions and the sad outcome for deniers?—the untold sin, and suffering and eventual death of untold millions since the Eden Fall!

What incentive then, for determination to align oneself with and heartily follow and obey our good God's will and law! And this was exactly what Christ, Who thus obeyed His Father implicitly, initiated with His followers, as we see by the following.

"Jesus spoke these words, lifted up His eyes to heaven, and said: Father...I have finished the work which You have given Me to do...I have manifested Your name to the men whom You have given Me...and they have kept Your word...For I have given to them the words which You have given to Me, and they have received them...I do not pray that You should take them out of the world, but that You should keep them from the evil one...Sanctify them by Your truth—Your Word is truth" (John 17:1–17).

How simple, the gospel truth and plan of salvation, reader. It is thus to, through the sanctifying Savior, believe and receive and obey the Word of God, and, a grace-given sanctified life thus will keep you from evil and the evil one, and in the end see you gain eternal life. What incentive to "trust and obey" as the good hymn says.

And how heartening, reader, that as by great Paul the gospel was thus preached, many did believe the Word and savingly turn from sin and Satan to the Savior. Listen: "Then Paul, as his custom was, went in to them, and for three Sabbaths reasoned with them from the Scriptures...and a great multitude of the devout Greeks, and not a few of the leading women, joined Paul and Silas." (Acts 17:2–4).

And though, reader, this caused jealous dissention among the Jews and the departing of Paul, still, the spreading thus of the gospel truth soon found others who did believe and obey the Word. Listen: "Then the brethren immediately sent Paul and Silas away by night to Berea. When they arrived, they went into the synagogue of the Jews. These were more fair-minded than those in Thessalonica, in that they received the Word with all readiness, and searched the Scriptures daily to find out whether these things were so. Therefore many of them believed" (Acts 17:10–12).

And that this was no exception reader, thus continuing the spread of the saving Word of God, we see by Paul's following account. "You yourselves know, brethren, that our coming to you was not in vain...we were bold to in our God to speak to you the gospel of God...that you would walk worthy of God, Who calls you into His Own kingdom and glory.

For this reason we also thank God without ceasing, because when you received the Word of God which you heard from us, you welcomed it not as the word of men, but as it is in truth, the Word of God, which also effectively works in you who believe" (1 Thess. 2:1, 2, 12, 13).

And the apostle Peter, reader, agrees concerning this saving power of the received and obeyed Word, as follows. "Since you have purified your souls in obeying the truth through the Spirit in sincere love of the brethren, love one another fervently with a pure heart, having been born again...through the Word of God which lives and abides forever...the Word which by the gospel was preached to you" (1 Pet. 22–25).

Then the apostle advises those thus reborn, as follows, reader. "Therefore, laying aside all...as newborn babes, desire the pure milk of the Word, that you may grow thereby...having your conduct honorable among the Gentiles, that when they speak against you as evildoers, they may, by your good works which they observe, glorify God...

For to this you were called, because Christ also suffered for us, leaving us an example, that you should follow His steps, Who committed no sin...Who Himself bore our sins in His Own body on the tree, that we, having died to sins, might live for righteousness" (1 Pet. 2:1, 2, 12, 21–24).

And he concludes reader, cautioning: "Therefore humble yourselves under the mighty hand of God, that He may exalt you in due time, casting all your care upon Him, for He cares for you. Be sober, be vigilant; because your adversary the devil walks about like a roaring lion, seeking whom he may devour. Resist him steadfast in the faith" (1 Pet. 5:6–9).

And Peter, reader, well knows whereof he warns—for, the devil did trip him up just as Christ had warned him. But, with broken-hearted and tearful repentance, Peter returned to his forgiving Savior, and ever after proved his repentance in a life of total servitude for his Lord.

And how grateful we should be, reader, that in the all-providing Word, we have such encouraging and guiding examples. And not only that, but also full and encouraging directives the following of which, like with the worthies of old, can and will bring us off "more than conquerors."

For pertinent example, reader, listen: "Finally, my brethren, be strong in the Lord and in the power of His might. Put on the whole armor of God, that you may be able to stand against the wiles of the devil. For we do not wrestle against flesh and blood, but against principalities, against powers, against the rulers of the darkness of this age, against spiritual hosts of wickedness in the heavenly places.

Therefore, take up the whole armor of God, that you may be able to withstand in the evil day, and having done all, to stand. Stand therefore, having girded your waist with truth, having put on the breastplate of righteousness, and having shod your feet with the preparation of the gospel of peace; above all, taking the shield of faith with which you will be able to quench all the fiery darts of the wicked one. And take the helmet of salvation, and the sword of the Spirit, which is the Word of God" (Eph. 6:10–17).

Sounds like preparation for spiritual warfare, reader!—and, of course, that is exactly what the Christian is engaged in. But, again, how more than good that, thus equipping ourself, we can be sure, under and by God, of complete victory. And the great spiritual warrior Paul, indeed gives just such encouragement, asserting: "The sting of death is sin, and the strength of sin is the law. But thanks be to God, Who gives us the victory through our Lord Jesus Christ" (1 Cor. 15:56–57).

And then he follows this up showing on our part, the winning method, saying: "But you must continue in the things which you have learned and been assured of, knowing...you have known the Holy Scriptures, which are able to make you wise for salvation through faith in Christ Jesus. All Scripture is given by inspiration of God, and is profitable for doctrine, for reproof, for correction, for instruction in righteousness, that the man of God may be complete, thoroughly equipped for every good work" (2 Tim. 3:14–17).

So it's plain, reader, that God has done His necessary part in supplying all our needs for life and salvation, and therefore now it's for us to do our part therein. As the prophet Moses said: "The secret things belong to the Lord our God, but those things which are revealed (by the Word), belong to us and to our children forever, that we may do all the words of this law (meaning the revealed Scriptures)" (Deut. 29:29).

And Paul agreeingly adds: "For whatever things were written before were written for our learning, that we through the patience and comfort of the Scriptures might have hope...according to the commandment of the everlasting God for obedience to the faith" (Rom. 15:4; 16:26). And the apostle James adds as follows.

Every good gift and every perfect gift is from above, and comes down from the Father...of His Own will He brought us forth by the Word of truth...Therefore lay aside all filthiness and overflow of wickedness, and receive with meekness the implanted Word, which is able to save your souls. But, be doers of the Word, and not hearers only...he who looks into the perfect law of liberty and continues in it, and is not a forgetful hearer, but a doer of the work, this one will be blessed in what he does" (James 1:17–25).

And similarly, reader, again reminding us we are in a spiritual battle, Paul adds as follows. "You therefore must endure hardship as a good soldier of Jesus Christ. No one engaged in warfare entangles himself with the affairs of this life, that he may please Him who enlisted him as a soldier...Be diligent to present yourself approved to God, a worker who does not need to be ashamed, rightly dividing the Word of truth" (2 Tim. 2:3, 4, 15).

God's Key To Savingly Understanding His Word

So here, reader, as a scripturally designated directive in following the holy and obedient life desribed and called for, Paul lastly adds a new key to doing so—that of "rightly dividing the Word." Therefore, in order to achieve this obedient and saving holiness, you will agree, we need to comprehend just what rightly dividing the Word means.

And where, reader, would we look for the answer—but to God's Word itself? And in this investigation, we need to recall that this miracle Book was written over a period of say 1,500 years by about forty divinely-inspired writers—yet all indeed miraculously integrated! So, herein we see that God's Truth, which is obviously progressive in revelation, necessarily then, calls for it to be carefully dissected—or, "rightly divided."

In other words, reader, the Word is not like a regular story book that can be read through from first to last as a continuously unfolding story. Rather, since there are many continuing "installments" thereof, a complete picture of Truth will only be found by searching it throughout for light on its various topics.

And that, reader, is the aforementioned "rightly dividing" of Scripture. And thus it is that the apostle Paul agreeingly asserts as follows. "The Spirit searches all things, yes, the deep things of God...Now we have received, not the spirit of the world, but the Spirit Who is from God, that we might know the things that have been freely given to us of God. These things we also speak, not in words which man's wisdom teaches, but which the Holy Spirit teaches, comparing spiritual things with spiritual" (1 Cor. 2:10–14).

Plain then, reader, that in order to arrive at a consensus of the truth on any subject, we do so by comparing and collating that found thereon throughout the Word. And here as follows is the way the Spirit had the "gospel prophet" describe it. "Whom will He teach knowledge? And whom will He make to understand the message?...precept must be upon precept, precept upon precept, line upon line, line upon line, here a little, there a little...the Word of the Lord was to them, "precept upon precept, precept upon precept, line upon line, line upon line, here a little, there a little" (Isa.28:9–13).

And repetance, as here, reader, scripturally expresses the importance of that revealed. But, of course, in all fairness, it needs to be seen that indeed this is authenticated by such use scripturally, including that of the New Testament as well. And, true to His Word, reader—notice how this described method of "rightly dividing" and so teaching scriptural truth, indeed is used by the Lord Himself.

Listen: "Jesus came to Nazareth, where He had been brought up. And as His custom was, He went into the synagogue on the Sabbath day, and stood up to read. And He was handed the book of the prophet Isaiah. And when He had opened the book, He found the place where it was written: "The Spirit of the Lord is upon Me, because He has anointed Me to preach the gospel"...Then He closed the book, and...He began to say to them, "Today this Scripture is fulfilled in your hearing." So all bore witness to Him" (Luke 4:16–22).

So here, reader, we see a plain application by the Savior of the "line upon line, here a little, there a little" system of "rightly dividing" Scripture. And that this also was a custom of His, notice as follows: "Then He said to them, "O foolish ones, and slow of heart to believe in all that the prophets have spoken! Ought not Christ to have suffered these things and to enter into His glory?"

And beginning at Moses and all the Prophets, He expounded to them in all the Scriptures the things concerning Himself...Then He said to them, "These are the words which I spoke to you while I was still with you, that all things must be fulfilled which were written in the Law of Moses and the Prophets and the Psalms concerning Me." And He opened their understanding, that they might comprehend the Scriptures. Then He said to them, "Thus it is written, and thus it was necessary for the Christ to suffer and to rise from the dead the third day" (Luke 24:25–27;44–46).

A lesson from Christ Himself and His Word, reader, on rightly dividing the Scriptures, showing how that putting line upon line and here a little and there a little, we can thus come to comprehend them and their various subjects, thus gaining an understanding thereof.

And just here, in this ever so plain example of this Scripture-comprehending system, illustrated by Christ Himself, He pinpoints the very heart of the Scriptures—the Savior Himself. That He Himself and His saving mission to us fallen sinners is indeed the center subject thereof, He makes plain also in His following assertion.

Listen as He addresses the Jews: "You search the Scriptures, for in them you think you have eternal life—and these are they which testify of Me. But you are not willing to come to Me that you may have life...there is one who accuses you—Moses, in whom you trust. For if you believed Moses, you would believe Me, for he wrote about Me" (John 5:39–46). So again, reader, here is another Christ-given example of rightly dividing Scripture, beside revealing again that Christ is the central subject in Scripture, indeed, the very sum and substance thereof.

And, the disciples themselves accord with this fact and system, it being the very means by which they were able to recognize Him as the long-promised Messiah. As John further delineates, listen: "John (the Baptist) bore witness of Him and cried out, saying, "This was He of Whom I said, 'He Who comes after me is preferred before me, for He was before me...For the law was given through Moses, but grace and truth came through Jesus Christ...

I am the voice of one crying in the wilderness: "make straight the way of the Lord," as the prophet Isaiah said"...The next day John saw Jesus coming toward him and said, "Behold!—the Lamb of God Who takes away the sin of the world...He Who sent me to baptize with water said to me, 'Upon Whom you see the Spirit descending, and remaining on Him, this is He Who baptizes with the Holy Spirit.' And I have seen and testified that this is the Son of God...And Philip found Nathanael and said to him, "We have found Him of Whom Moses in the Law, and also the prophets, wrote—Jesus of Nazareth" (John 1:15–17, 23, 32–34, 45).

And notice following, reader, how as Jesus claimed to be the central subject of Scripture, the disciples, seeing how this indeed fit with the Scriptures, wholly agreed therewith. "Then they (the Jews) said to Him, "What shall we do, that we may work the works of God?" Jesus answered and said to them, "This is the work of God, that you believe in Him Whom He sent...It is written in the prophets 'And they shall all be taught by God'...It is the Spirit Who gives life; the flesh profits nothing. The words that I speak to you are spirit, and they are life"...Simon Peter answered Him, "Lord, to whom shall we go? You have the words of eternal life. Also, we have come (thereby) to believe and know that You are the Christ, the Son of the living God" (John 6:28, 29, 45, 63, 68, 69).

Further, reader, John not only thus points to Christ as the central subject of the Word, but even declares Him—Who is all in all—to in essence be "the Word." Listen: "In the beginning was the Word, and the Word was with God, and the Word was God...as many as received Him, to them He gave the right to become children of God, to those who believe in His name, who were born...of God. And the Word became flesh and dwelt among us" (John 1:1, 12–14).

So again, reader, here we see that those who accept that Christ is the Scripture-promised Savior and believe in and accept Him as such, are savingly born as "children of God." And This is further accented as follows: "Most assuredly, I say to you, he who hears My word and believes in Him Who sent Me, has everlasting life" (John 5:24). And: "And this is the will of Him Who sent Me, that everyone who sees the Son and believes in Him, may have everlasting life...therefore everyone who has heard and learned from the Father comes to Me...Most assuredly, I say to you, he who believes in Me has everlasting life" (John 6:40, 45, 47).

So by all such, reader, it is plain that to gain everlasting life, it is necessary on our part to believe the Word, and in Christ, the scripturally-promised living Word, as our Savior. Recall: "For this reason we also thank God without ceasing, because when you received the Word of God which you heard from us, you welcomed it, not as the word of men, but as it is in truth, the Word of God, which also effectively works in you who believe" (1 Thes. 2:13).

So plainly, reader, the key to having the Word, and thus the Living Word, effectively work savingly in us, is for us to exercise faith and believe to that end. And the apostle Paul nails it down, saying: "Now faith is the substance of things hoped for, the evidence of things (salvation) not seen. For by it the elders obtained a good testimony...But, without faith it is impossible to please Him, for he who comes to God must believe that He is, and that He is a rewarder of those who diligently seek Him" (Heb. 11:1–6).

Surely then reader, since faith is the paramount key to having and living the saved life, we will want to know how it is obtained. And as Peter formerly attested that Christ had "the words of eternal life", certainly we can have faith that in that Word is where we will savingly be pointed to faith's source.

Listen as Paul further enlightens hereon in face of God's offer of salvation: "I beseech you therefore, brethren, by the mercies of God, that you present your bodies a living sacrifice, holy, acceptable to God...For I say...God has dealt to each one a measure of faith" (Rom. 12:1–3). So again, reader, just like salvation itself, the faith to gain it by, is a God-given gift!

And now, in his law-like fashion, Paul goes on to show just how we come to gain this valuable gift that brings a saved and righteous life. Listen: "The righteousness of faith speaks in this way..."The Word is near you, in your mouth and in your heart"—that is, the Word of faith which we preach: that if you confess with your mouth the Lord Jesus and believe in your heart that God has raised Him from the dead, you will be saved. For with the heart one believes unto righteousness, and with the mouth confession is made unto salvation. For the

Scripture says…"Whoever calls on the name of the Lord shall be saved" (Rom. 10:6–13).

So notice here again, reader, how lawyer Paul always systematically draws his material from Scripture, a little here and a little there. And similarly, the apostle John agreeingly adds as follows. Listen: "Whoever believes that Jesus is the Christ is born of God…For whoever is born of God overcomes the world. And this is the victory that has overcome the world—even our faith" (1 John 5:1, 4). This then, reader, is the Word's faith-way to "righteousness by faith."

And God's Word throughout, encouragingly and manifoldly agrees. For example, listen as the Psalmist delineates: "How can a young man cleanse his way? By taking heed according to Your Word…Your Word have I hidden in my heart, that I might not sin against You…Let Your mercies come also to me, O Lord—Your salvation, according to Your Word. For I trust in Your Word" (Ps. 119:9–11, 41, 42).

And the gospel prophet adds: "Listen to Me, you who follow after righteousness, you who seek the Lord…For a law will proceed from Me, and I will make My justice rest as a light of the peoples. My righteousness is near, My salvation has gone forth, and My arms will judge the peoples, and on My arm they will trust" (Isa. 51:1, 4, 5).

And His Word gives the following encouragement to the believer, reader: "The Lord is good, a stronghold in the day of trouble—and He knows those who trust in Him" (Nah. 1:7)—"trust" simply being faith exercised as belief. And speaking of trusting the Lord and His Word, Paul encourages: "Godliness is profitable for all things, having promise for the life that now is and of that which is to come…trust in the living God, Who is the Savior of all men, especially of those who believe" (1 Tim. 4:8–10).

Now the Lord has given us a living example of all such, reader, in the life experience of the patriarch Abraham—the trusting one through whom He promised the Messiah-Savior would come. This, of course, because of Abraham's faith and dutiful, trusting obedience to God. And it is him whom Paul uses as a special illustration and example of this "righteousness by faith" of which we have studied.

Listen: "What does the Scripture say? "Abraham believed God, and it was accounted to him for righteousness."...Therefore it is of faith that it might be according to grace, so that the promise might be sure to all...those who are of the faith of Abraham, who is the father of us all...

And not being weak in faith, he did not consider his own body, already dead, since he was about a hundred years old, and the deadness of Sarah's womb. He did not waver at the promise of God (of yet having a child) through unbelief, but was strengthened in faith, giving glory to God, and being fully convinced that what He had promised, He was also able to perform.

And therefore, "it was accounted to him for righteousness." Now it was not written for his sake alone that it was imputed to him, but also for us. It shall be imputed to us who believe in Him Who raised up Jesus our Lord from the dead, Who was delivered up because of our offenses, and was raised for our justification" (Rom. 4:3, 16–25).

And so from Paul's real-life lesson application, reader—since our faith needs to equate that of Abraham to be saving faith—we need to learn about his faith. Listen: "Now the Lord had said to Abram: "Get out of your country, from your family and father's house, to a land that I will show you. I will make you a great nation...and in you all the families of the earth shall be blessed." So Abram departed as the Lord had spoken to him, and Lot went with him. And Abram was seventy-five years old when he departed" (Gen. 12:1–4).

No small requirement, reader!—and no small faith on Abram's part either, especially in that, as it says elsewhere "he went out not knowing where he was going." And this especially in that he had no child yet to carry his family-race on in order to fulfill God's prophecy-promise—besides his being now 75 years old!

So—"After these things the word of the Lord came to Abram, saying, "Do not be afraid, Abram. I am your shield, your exceedingly great reward. But Abram said, "Lord God, what will You give me, seeing I go childless?...You have given me no offspring...And behold, the word of the Lord came to him, saying, "one who will come from your own body shall be your heir."

Then He brought him outside and said, "Look now toward heaven, and count the stars if you are able to number them—so shall your descendants be." And he believed the Lord, and He accounted (imputed) it to him for righteousness" (Gen. 15:1–6). Good thing, reader—because as the years dragged on, at times Abram's faith grew slim. And, it was not until he was a hundred years old, that finally the Lord did give him a son and heir!

But when the lad was maturing, reader, then came the greatest test of his faith of all. Listen: "Now it came to pass after these things that God tested Abraham, and said to him, "Abraham!" And he said, "Here I am." Then He said, "Take now your son, your only son, Isaac, whom you love, and go to the land of Moriah, and offer him there as a burnt offering on one of the mountains of which I shall tell you."

Talk about a test of faith, reader!—but by now Abram's faith in his Lord had matured to the place that it stood this self-crucifying test. For, this dutiful servant of God had gone the length—he had made the altar, put on the wood, then bound willing Isaac and laid him thereon, yes, and had even raised the sacrificial knife—but listen!

"But the Angel of the Lord called to him from heaven and said, "Abraham, Abraham!" So he said, "Here I am." And He said, "Do not lay your hand on the lad, or do anything to him; for now I know that you fear God, since you have not withheld your son, your only son, from Me...By Myself I have sworn, says the Lord, because you have done this thing, and have not withheld your son, your only son...In your seed all the nations of the earth shall be blessed, because you have obeyed My voice" (Gen. 22:1–18).

Talk about faith and trust, reader!—and notice that it is plainly shown hereby that obedience naturally issues from this kind of genuine faith-trust. This above setting and resulting promise, then, is patently a New Covenant or Testament one obviously, since it entailed the spiritual blessing of all mankind through the promised "seed of the woman" Messiah-Savior. Yes, herein we see that it is the genuine obedient New Covenant faith-trust that carries right over into the New Testament itself.

Listen then from that source: "By faith Abraham obeyed when he was called to go out to the place which he would receive as an inheritance. And he went out, not knowing where he was going. By faith he dwelt in the land of promise as in a foreign country, dwelling in tents with Isaac and Jacob, the heirs with him of the same promise...

By faith Abraham, when he was tested, offered up Isaac, and he who had received the promises offered up his only begotten son, of whom it was said, "In Isaac your seed shall be called," he concluding that God was able to raise him up, even from the dead, from which he also received him in a figurative sense" (Heb.11:8-10,17-19). No wonder he was called "the father of the faithful"—those full of faith, reader!

And Paul, adds the application to such, saying: "Abraham "believed God, and it was accounted to him for righteousness." Therefore know that only those who are of faith are sons of Abraham. And the Scripture, foreseeing that God would justify the Gentiles by faith, preached the gospel to Abraham beforehand, saying, "In you all the nations shall be blessed." So then, those who are of faith are blessed with believing Abraham...Now to Abraham and his Seed were the promises made. He does not say "And to seeds," as of many, but as of one, "And to your Seed," Who is Christ" (Gal. 3:6–9, 16).

So how gracious of our good God, reader, as with Abraham, to also account us New Covenant saving status through believing by faith—yet, genuine trusting and obedient faith. And also, do you see by Paul's above revelation concerning Abraham's similarly being accepted as "the gospel was preached" to him, that salvation came back in Old Testament days also by grace through faith and belief just as now in New Covenant or Testament days?

Further, reader, do you also see from the above, that salvation by faith through grace comes by and through God's one and only Provision—the "Seed of the woman", the long-promised Messiah, Christ our Savior? Just as Paul further adds in the above citation in Galatians, saying as follows.

"But the Scripture has confined all under sin, that the promise by faith in Jesus Christ might be given to those who believe...Therefore the law (OT) was our tutor to bring us to Christ, that we might be justified by faith...For you are all sons of God through faith in Christ Jesus...And if you are Christ's, then you are Abraham's seed, and heirs according to the promise" (Gal. 3:22–29).

Along with Paul's assertion, reader, that we are "justified by faith in Christ"—that is, thus accepted as righteous before a holy God and Law—notice how he further confirms this in Abraham's experience, as follows. "He did not waver at the promise of God through unbelief, but...being fully convinced that what He had promised He was also able to perform. And therefore, "it was accounted to him for righteousness."

Now it was not written for His sake alone that it was imputed to him, but also for us. It shall be imputed to us who believe in Him Who raised up Jesus our Lord from the dead, Who was delivered up because of our offenses, and was raised for our justification" (Rom. 4:20–25).

What mercy, reader, that sets the captives of sin free!—as they believingly accept that the Savior died on Calvary's cruel cross to atone for their sins. Yes, and that a gracious God thus through their believing acceptance that He does thus become their personal Savior from sin, is able to and does thus "justify" them—accept them as righteous before Him and His holy Law.

And notice how Paul further, reader, confirmingly backs this all up as follows, thus showing just how He could rightly "justify" one thus. Listen: "This righteousness from God comes through faith in Jesus Christ to all who believe. There is no difference, for all have sinned and fall short of the glory of God, and are justified freely by His grace through the redemption that came by Christ Jesus.

God presented Him as a sacrifice of atonement, through one having faith in His blood...He did this to demonstrate His justice at the present time, so as to be just, as the One Who justifies the man who has faith in Jesus" (Rom. 3:22–26 NIV). And so again, reader, when one by faith believes that, though totally undeserving, Christ died in his place on Calvary's cruel cross to pay for his sins, and receives Him as his Savior from sin, that one is justly counted as justified before God and His holy Law. So now that he is forgiven for disobeying God and His Law, and has a second chance, reader, would not that one naturally be expected to henceforth gladly obey God and His law of love? Paul certainly asserts so as he carries on, saying as follows.

Listen: "Do we then make void the law through faith? Certainly not! On the contrary, we establish the law" (Rom. 3:31). Paul's reasoning is crystal clear reader—he plainly infers that since it cost the very Life of God to be able to satisfy the demand of the law for our forfeited lives, that most certainly shows that obedience to God and His holy Law is supremely essential. Indeed—God would die, rather than change His holy law!

And this is exactly what he further now asserts as follows. Listen: "What shall we say then? Shall we continue in sin that grace may abound? Certainly not! How shall we who died to sin live any longer in it?...For if we have been united together in the likeness of His death, certainly we also shall be in the likeness of His resurrection, knowing that our old man (life) was crucified with Him, that the body of sin might be done away with, that we should no longer be slaves of sin...

For the death that He died, He died to sin once for all; but the life He lives, He lives to God. Likewise you also reckon yourselves to be dead indeed to sin, but alive to God in Christ Jesus our Lord...For sin shall not have dominion over you, for you are not under law, but under grace...

But God be thanked that though you were slaves of sin, yet you obeyed from the heart that form of doctrine to which you were delivered. And having been set free from sin, you became slaves of righteousness...Now having been set free from sin, and having become slaves of God, you have your fruitage to holiness, and the end—everlasting life" (Rom. 6:1–22).

The new Christ-life, reader!—and, typically, Paul goes on to pinpoint it's modus operandi, it's empowering. Listen: "There is therefore now no condemnation to those who are in Christ Jesus, who do not walk according to the flesh, but according to the Spirit. For the law of the Spirit of life in Christ Jesus has made me free from the law of sin and death.

For what the law could not do in that it was weak through the flesh, God did by sending His Own Son in the likeness of sinful flesh, on account of sin. He condemned sin in the flesh, that the righteous requirements of the law, might be fulfilled in us who do not walk according to the flesh, but according to the Spirit...And if Christ is in you, the body is dead because of sin, but the Spirit is life because of righteousness" (Rom. 8:1–4, 10).

The Justifier Also Savingly Sanctifies

No wonder this all is called "so great salvation", reader—wherein, by the sinner repentantly accepting Christ as Savior from sin by faith, the Savior forgivingly cleanses and saves him from his former sins and sinfulness—thus God being able to account him as righteous or "justified" before Him and His holy Law. And, praise God, this also delivering him from habitual sinning in the future—this as by the ever-present Spirit of Christ, the Savior lives His holy life within him in the newly-begun life of "sanctification."

And Christ Himself, reader, made all this plain to persecuting Saul-Paul as he went about furthering such. Listen: "Saul, Saul...I am Jesus Whom you are persecuting. But...I now send you to open their eyes, in order to turn them from darkness to light, and from the power of Satan to God, that they may receive forgiveness of sins, and an inheritance among those who are sanctified by faith in Me" (Acts 26:14–18).

So, reader, by this we see that sanctification, like justification, is also by faith—by faith in Christ as Savior, of course. And just here lies the much-needed answer to the much-experienced problem of people confusing these works as legalism. Yes, this to the point of erroneously looking upon sanctification's scripturally-sanctioned "good works" as such! And the answer to this confusion and enigma, reader, is, of course, to be found as we let Scripture give its own answer. And this is satisfactorily done as we allow God's Word to show who, in sanctification's good works, is doing the works. And this was Christ's great demonstration hereon in all of His numberless "good works" all the way from childhood through His life here on earth.

Yes, reader, He Himself cleared up this error of equating sanctified good works with legalism in making clear just who was doing the works. Listen!: "I can of myself do nothing...I do not seek My Own will, but the will of the Father Who sent Me" (John 5:30). And: "believe that I am in the Father, and the Father in Me...The Father Who dwells in Me does the works. Believe Me that I am in the Father and the Father in Me" (John 14:10, 11).

And, if we will only let God's good Word give the truth on this divisive matter, reader, there is no legalism in sanctified good works at all! For example, listen again to Paul: "Therefore, my beloved, as you have always obeyed (not legalistically!)...work out your own salvation with fear and trembling; for it is God Who works in you both to will and to do for His good pleasure...that you may become blameless and harmless, children of God without fault...holding fast the Word of life" (Phil. 2:12–16).

So we see the answer to this confusing matter of supposed legalism, reader, as we notice that it is God's good works done in us. And addressing the saints, Paul there further says of them: "being confident of this very thing, that He Who has begun a good work in you, will complete it until the day of Jesus Christ" (Phil. 1:6). Thus we further, see here, reader, that being sanctified is a progressive work of the Lord in you—right up to the end.

And notice how Paul continues to make this plain and to tie these various manifestations of sanctification together. Listen as addressing the believers as brethren beloved of the Lord, he adds: "God from the beginning chose you for salvation through sanctification by the Spirit (His work) and belief in the truth (your work), to which He called you by our gospel for the obtaining of the glory of our Lord Jesus" (2 Thes. 2:13, 14).

And writing to these same saints, reader, Paul adds further, again pointing out plainly Who is doing the doing! Listen: "Now may the God of peace Himself sanctify you completely...preserved blameless unto the coming of our Lord Jesus Christ. He Who calls you is faithful, Who also will do it" (1 Thes. 5:23, 24).

And, reader, wanting it to be seen that, as seen here, sanctification, beginning immediately following justification, is a continuing work of the Lord by His Spirit in us, Paul adds as follows. Listen: "in bringing many sons to glory...both he Who sanctifies and those who are being sanctified are all of one, for which reason He is not ashamed to call them brethren" (Heb. 3:11).

How like our gracious and longsuffering Lord-God, reader—that He doesn't expect or require the new Christian to at once be fully complete. And all of the above revelations fit perfectly with Scripture's similar simile of likening the newly justified and so born again Christian to an infant—perfect at that initial stage, but needing growth and maturing.

This such as is encouraged, saying as follows. "As newborn babes, desire the pure milk of the Word, that you may grow thereby, if indeed you have tasted that the Lord is gracious"—"You therefore, beloved...grow in the grace and knowledge of our Lord and Savior, Jesus Christ" (1 Pet. 2:2, 3; 2 Pet. 3:18).

And Paul, reader, again pinpoints the medium whereby we thus maturingly grow, as follows. "So now, brethren, I commend you to God and to the Word of His grace, which is able to build you up and give you an inheritance among all those who are sanctified" (Acts 20:32). And later, he urges further as follows.

Listen: "Finally, brethren, we urge and exhort in the Lord Jesus that you should abound more and more just as you received from us how you ought to walk and to please God...for this is the will of God, even your sanctification...that each of you should know how to possess his own vessel in sanctification and honor" (1 Thes.4:1–4).

So here the Word, reader, as in many other places, likens the Christian life to a "walk" with the Lord. And His promise is that as we so walk: "Your ears shall hear a word behind you, saying, "This is the way, walk in it," whenever you turn to the right hand or whenever you turn to the left" (Isa. 30:21).

Good, reader—but, the problem is that at times for one reason or another, we just stray off course a bit—right? Well, just like the more than gracious Lord-God He is, He has help for that problem too. And why?—because their slips and falls are not done wilfully, they do not "practice" sin, that is, live a life of continual, wilful rebellion against God and His holy law—for, that is what "sin" really is.

No, they at times just trip and slip—maybe by a "slip of the lip" or such—and for just such the good Lord has coverage—whereas with the wilfully rebellious, it is different. Listen: "A righteous man may fall seven times and rise again—but the wicked shall fall by calamity" (Prov. 24:16).

And the Psalmist, reader, adds: "The steps of a good man are ordered by the Lord, and He delights in his way. Though he falls, he shall not be utterly cast down, for the Lord upholds him with His hand...For the Lord loves justice, and does not forsake His saints...the law of his God is in his heart; none of his steps shall slide" (Ps. 37:23, 24, 28, 31).

Not that the righteous who slip or fall try to cover up their sins, reader, nor yet does their good God. No, they are rather quick to recognize their failures and sins and repentantly make amends according to God's Word. The Psalmist makes this plain as follows.

"I acknowledged my sin to You O Lord, and my iniquity I have not hidden. I said, "I will confess my transgressions to the Lord," and You forgave the iniquity of my sin...Blessed is he whose transgression is forgiven, whose sin is covered. Blessed is the man to whom the Lord does not impute iniquity, and in whose spirit there is no deceit" (Ps. 32:5, 1, 2).

And John the beloved, reader, adds: "My little children, these things I write to you, so that you may not sin. And, if anyone sins, we have an Advocate with the Father, Jesus Christ the righteous. And He Himself is the propitiation (sacrifice) for our sins" ...If we walk in the light as He is in the light, we have fellowship with one another, and the blood of Jesus Christ His Son cleanses us from all sin...If we confess our sins, He is faithful and just to forgive us our sins and to cleanse us from all unrighteousness" (1 John 2:1, 2; 1:7, 9).

So we notice lastly here, reader, that "sin" is "unrighteousness"—obviously, then, righteousness, sin's opposite, is to not sin and not break God's law. And John plainly states: "sin is lawlessness"; "sin is the transgression of the law" (1 John 3:4, KJV). So, reader—it is axiomatic then that righteousness is lawfulness and lawkeeping. And the Psalmist agreeingly adds as follows.

Listen: "Righteous are You, O Lord, and upright are Your judgements...Your righteousness is an everlasting righteousness, and Your law is truth...and all Your commandments are truth...great peace have those who love Your law, and nothing causes them to stumble...for all Your commandments are righteousness" (Ps. 119:137, 142, 151, 165, 172).

So it's more than plain, reader, that the way to righteousness is the keeping of His law by grace. And nothing could be more plain from the testimony of His holy Word. For trite example, listen as it describes the lifestyle of righteous John the Baptist's similarly righteous parents as follows. "There was a certain priest named Zacharias...His wife was of the daughters of Aaron and her name was Elizabeth. And they were both righteous before God, walking in all the commandments and ordinances of the Lord blameless" (Luke 1:5, 6).

No, reader—a just God does not ask the impossible by asking us to keep His commandments, but has given power through Him to do so. And this is exactly what the apostle Paul calls us all to, saying as follows. "Do not be deceived: "Evil company corrupts good habits. "Awake to righteousness and do not sin" (1 Cor. 15:33, 34). And he further describes this as the lifestyle of Christ Himself as the Father says to Him as follows. Listen: "Your throne, O God, is forever and ever; a scepter of righteousness is the scepter of Your kingdom. You have loved righteousness and hated lawlessness" (Heb. 1:8, 9).

And we read further of Him, reader: "Christ also suffered for us, leaving us an example, that you should follow His steps, Who committed no sin...Who Himself bore our sins in His Own body on the tree, that we, having died to sin, might live for righteousness" (1 Pet. 2:21–24). So sin being lawbreaking, the genuine Christian, who follows his or her Savior, reader, puts it away by keeping God's holy Law through grace.

And John the beloved, who leaned close on Jesus breast and lived thus for Him, agreeingly adds as follows. "And now, little children, abide in Him, that when He appears, we may have confidence and not be ashamed before Him at His coming. If you know that He is righteous, you know that everyone who practices righteousness is born of Him" (1 John 2:28, 29).

So it is plain, reader, that Christ's born-again followers righteously and obediently keep His law. And John makes this patently plain as follows. "Whoever commits sin also commits lawlessness, and sin is lawlessness (the transgression of the law, KJV). And you know that He was manifested to take away our sins—and in Him there is no sin...

Little children, let no one deceive you—he who practices righteousness is righteous, just as He is righteous...Whoever has been born of God does not (practice) sin...In this the children of God and the children of the devil are manifest—whoever does not practice righteousness is not of God... Beloved, if our heart does not condemn us, we have confidence toward God. And whatever we ask we receive from Him because we keep His commandments...Now he who keeps His commandments abides in Him, and He in him. And by this we know that He abides in us, by the Spirit Whom He has given us" (3:4–10,20–24).

So plainly then, reader—the Holy Spirit is given to those who by practice obey God and keep His commandments. And we see this fact corroborated as follows. Listen: "Peter and the other apostles answered (the Jewish leaders) and said: "We ought to obey God rather than men. The God of our fathers raised up Jesus...and we are His witnesses to these things, and so also is the Holy Spirit Whom God has given to those who obey Him" (Acts 5:32). Yes, this is the "Spirit of Christ", reader, through Whom Christ lives His holy and obedient, lawkeeping life within us.

And Christ also made this plain, saying: "If you love Me keep My commandments. And I will pray the Father and He will give you another Helper, that He may abide with you forever—the Spirit of truth...you know Him for He dwells with you and will be in you. (In this way) I will not leave you orphans—I will come to you...He who has My commandments and keeps them...I will love him and manifest Myself to him" (John 14:15–21).

Further: "It is to your advantage that I go away, for...if I depart, I will send Him (the Spirit) to you. And when He has come, He will convict the world of sin (the breaking of God's law), and of righteousness (keeping God's law by grace), and of judgement...because the ruler (Satan) of this world is judged" (16:7, 8, 11).

And so, reader, thus keeping God's law holy by the presence and power of Christ through His Holy Spirit, such obedient ones He terms His "saints." Listen: "Here is the patience of the saints—here are those who keep the commandments of God and the faith of Jesus" (Rev. 14:12).

And, reader, the word "saints" in the original language is pertinently "holy ones." And so, in God's ordering and sight, as by the power of the holy Savior through His Holy Spirit they obey God and His holy Word and law, they are thus in the holy God's sight also accepted as being holy.

For recall, reader, Paul in Romans plainly states: "therefore, the law is holy, and the commandment holy and just and good" (Rom. 7:12). And he adds concerning such saintly holy ones: "But now having been set free from sin, and having become slaves of God, you have your fruitage to holiness, and the end—everlasting life" (6:22).

How perfectly wonderful, reader—since Paul affirms that "we shall all stand before the judgement seat of

Christ" (Rom. 14:10)—that we shall, as he further affirms, be able to do so holy and blameless! Listen: "Paul, an apostle of Jesus Christ by the will of God, to the saints...just as He chose us in Him before the foundation of the world, that we should be holy and without blame before Him" (Eph. 1:1–4).

And Paul, who doesn't mince his words when it comes to life and death matters, reader, sets the record straight as to the utter necessity of being thus, as he later says as follows. Listen: "Let us lay aside every weight and the sin which so easily ensnares us...looking unto Jesus, the author and finisher of our faith...For whom He loves He chastens...for our profit, that we may be partakers of His holiness...afterward it yields the peaceable fruitage of righteousness to those who have been trained by it. Therefore...pursue peace with all people, and holiness—without which, no one will see the Lord" (Heb. 12:1, 2, 10–14).

How supremely vital then, this holiness reader—without which we are lost! And pointedly, here Paul asserts that even Christ Himself, in His humanity, had to "go through this school of hard knocks" to this same end! Listen: "Who in the days of His flesh, when He had offered up prayers and supplications...was heard because of His godly fear. Though He was a Son, yet He learned obedience by the things which He suffered. And having been perfected, He became the author of eternal salvation to all who obey Him" (5:7–9).

Hence this urgent call to us, reader, saying: "elect...in sanctification of the Spirit, for obedience, and sprinkling of the blood of Christ...who are kept by the power of God through faith, for salvation ready to be revealed in the last time. In this you greatly rejoice, though now for a little while, if need be, you have been grieved by various trials...

Therefore, gird up the loins of your mind, be sober, and rest your hope fully upon the grace that is to be brought to you at the revelation of Jesus Christ, as obedient children, not conforming yourselves to the former lusts, as in your ignorance. But as He Who called you is holy, you also be holy in all your conduct, because it is written: "Be holy—for I am holy" (1 Pet. 1:1–6, 13–16).

How wonderful God's good plan of salvation, reader! For you notice above, that it rests fully upon God's good grace—and fully as wonderful is that as we willingly do put our full faith and trust in that saving grace, at the same time it empowers us to willingly obey God's holy law—we can't lose!

And this gives us overcoming courage, reader, to face Peter's further cautioning as, mingling these necessary elements to overcome, he continues the above. Listen: "The heavens and the earth which are now preserved by the same Word, are reserved for fire until the day of judgement and perdition of ungodly men...Therefore, since all these things will be dissolved, what manner of persons ought you to be in holy conduct and godliness, looking for and hastening the coming of the day of God...

Therefore, beloved, looking forward to these things, be diligent to be found by Him in peace, without spot and blameless" (3:7, 11–14). And as Ellen White encouraged, reader, typically, all of God's commands are enabling promises—promises of ability under Him to keep and fulfill the command.

But, how dreadful, reader, such requirement would be if its attainment was questionable and uncertain! But, in light of all we have seen and been assured of in God's holy Word as to its certain attainment by God's good grace—how encouragingly and blissfully wonderful!

How good that of God's obedient saints—when their number is fully made up and the harvest of the earth mentioned in the Revelation is completed—it will be able to be said of us as follows. "In that day this song will be sung..."We have a strong city (the New Jerusalem); God will appoint salvation for walls and bulwarks. Open the gates, that the righteous nation which keeps the truth may enter in" (Isa. 26:1, 2).

And in that great book of Revelation, reader, the completion of God's saving Word and Plan, it mentions that glorious city as follows. Listen: "Now I saw a new heaven and a new earth...Then I, John, saw the holy city, New Jerusalem, coming down out of heaven from God, prepared as a bride adorned for her husband...

Then He Who sat on the throne said, "Behold, I make all things new...He who overcomes shall inherit all things, and I will be his God and he shall be My son. But the cowardly, unbelieving, abominable, murderers, sexually immoral, sorcerers, idolaters, and all liars (the doubting disobedient!) shall have their part in the lake which burns with fire and brimstone, which is the second death...There shall by no means enter it anything that defiles, or causes an abomination or a lie, but only those who are written in the Lamb's Book of Life" (Rev. 21:1, 2, 7, 8).

And on the last page of the Word of God, reader, John adds concerning the end of probation as follows. "He who is unjust, let him be unjust still; he who is filthy, let him be filthy still; he who is righteous, let him be righteous still; he who is holy, let him be holy still...

"And behold, I am coming quickly, and My reward is with Me, to give every one according to his work...Blessed are those who do His commandments, that they may have the right to the tree of life, and may enter through the gates into the city.

But outside are dogs and sorcerers and sexually immoral and murderers and idolaters, and whoever loves and practices a lie (obviously symbolic, reader, for those who practice disobedience to God's holy law).

"I, Jesus, have sent My angel to testify to you these things in the churches. I am the Root and the Offspring of David, the bright and morning Star." And the Spirit and the bride (church) say, "Come!" And let him who hears say, "Come!" And let him who thirsts come. Whoever desires, let him take the water of Life freely" (22:11–17).

Reader—surely in all sanity, we would want to have all that glory with all eternity to enjoy it all with! Surely then what we need is the simple faith of a little child—or say of despised tax collector Zacchaeus, who, having heard Christ's gospel of love, on hearing He was to pass by, climbed up in a tree in order to see Him.

No doubt he felt Jesus would want nothing to do with him—but, not so! He Who reads the heart knew that here was a humble and repentant child of God wanting what his money could not supply—the Savior and salvation. And the great Lover of mankind supplied that to him that very day.

For, coming to that tree, He called him down and went home with him then and there. Showing he had let the gospel do its good work in his heart, Zacchaeus showed his obedience to God's law of love by saying to Jesus: "Lord, I give half my goods to the poor; and if I have taken anything from anyone by false accusation, I restore him fourfold."

And the gracious Savior replied: "Today salvation has come to this house, because he also is a son of (trusting and obedient) Abraham. For the Son of Man has come to seek and to save that which was lost" (Luke 19:8–10). And that which was lost which is promised to be restored, reader, includes all who will, praise our good and gracious God—and also as follows, much, much more!

All Lost By the Fall Is Bountifully Restored!

For, reader, a more than gracious Lord-God, in giving us the inestimable gift of life itself—recall—also "loaded us down with benefits", as it is written, as well! And so, in concluding our study, it would do us good to recall all that was lost of those benefits, so that we can in turn praise our good God for all He promises to restore to us His created children.

And so, reader, let us let the Word of Promise, by taking a little here and a little there, make a God-given promissory mosaic of all restored—

Life Itself—And this is the testimony: that God had given us eternal life, and this life is in His Son. He who has the Son has Life" (1 John 5:11, 12). "Do not fear any of those things which you are about to suffer. Indeed, the devil is about to throw some of you into prison...Be faithful unto death, and I will give you the crown of Life" (Rev. 2:10). "And He said to me..."I will give of the fountain of the water of Life freely to him who thirsts" (21:6).

Perfect Health—"Strengthen the weak hands, and make firm the feeble knees. Say to those who are fearful-hearted, "Be strong, do not fear!"...then the eyes of the blind shall be opened, and the ears of the deaf shall be unstopped. Then the lame shall leap like a deer, and the tongue of the dumb sing" (Isa. 35:3–6). "And God will wipe away every tear from their eyes; there shall be no more death, nor sorrow, nor crying. There shall be no more pain, for the former things have passed away" (Rev. 21:4).

103

Happiness to the Full—"I create new heavens and a new earth; and the former shall not be remembered or come to mind. But be glad and rejoice forever in what I create; for behold, I create Jerusalem a rejoicing, and her people a joy. I will rejoice in Jerusalem, and joy in My people, and the voice of weeping shall no longer be heard" (Isa. 65:17–19). "And the ransomed of the Lord shall return and come to Zion with singing, with everlasting joy on their heads. They shall obtain joy and gladness, and sorrow and sighing shall flee away" (35:10).

Edenic Mansion-homes—"They shall build houses and inhabit them; they shall plant vineyards and eat the fruit of them...For as the days of a tree shall be the days of My people, and My elect shall long enjoy the work of their hands" (Isa. 65:21, 22). "Let not your heart be troubled; you believe in God—believe also in Me. In My Father's house are many mansions...I go to prepare a place for you, and if I go and prepare a place for you, I will come again and receive you to Myself, that where I am, there you may be also" (John 14:1–3).

Gender and Culture Equality—"For you are all sons of God through faith in Christ Jesus...There is neither Jew nor Greek (Gentile), there is neither slave nor free, there is neither male nor female—for you are all one in Christ Jesus. And if you are Christ's, then you are Abraham's seed, and heirs according to the promise" (Gal. 3:26–28).

Dominion as Rulers—"So Jesus said to them, "Assuredly I say to you that in the regeneration, when the Son of Man sits on the throne of His glory, you who have followed Me will also sit on twelve thrones judging" (Matt. 19:28). "To him who overcomes I will grant to sit with Me on My throne, as I also overcame and sat down with My Father on His throne" (Rev. 3:21). "And I saw thrones, and they sat on them, and judgement was committed to them...Blessed and holy is he who has part in the first resurrection. Over such the second death has no power, but they shall be priests of God and of Christ, and shall reign with Him" (20:4, 6).

The Tree of Life—"To him who overcomes I will give to eat of the tree of Life, which is in the midst of the Paradise of God" (Rev. 2:7). "Blessed are those who do His commandments, that they may have the right to the tree of Life and may enter through the gates into the city" (22:14).

Everlasting Life—"Everyone who has left houses or brothers or sisters or father or mother or wife or children or lands, for My sake, shall receive a hundred-fold and inherit eternal Life" (Matt. 19:28, 29). "For God so loved the world that He gave His only begotten Son, that whoever believes in Him should not perish, but have everlasting Life" (John 3:16). "Jesus therefore answered and said to them..."Most assuredly I say to you, he who believes in Me has everlasting Life" (John 6:43, 47). "And this is the testimony: that God has given us eternal Life, and this Life is in His Son. He who has the Son has Life" (1 John 5:11, 12).

Perfection of Nature and Character—"And it shall come to pass that he who is left in Zion and remains in Jerusalem will be called holy...when the Lord has washed away the filth...and purged the blood of Jerusalem from her midst by the spirit of burning" (Isa.4:3, 4). "Open the gates that the righteous nation which keeps the truth may enter" (26:2). "The days of your mourning shall be ended. Also Your people shall all be righteous; they shall inherit the land forever" (60:20, 21). "The Gentiles shall see your righteousness...and they shall call them the holy people, the redeemed of the Lord" (62:2, 12).

Face To Face Communion With God!—"The desert shall rejoice and blossom as the rose...They shall see the glory of the Lord, the excellency of our God" (Isa. 35:1, 2). "Then I, John, saw the holy city, New Jerusalem, coming down out of heaven from God, prepared as a bride adorned for her husband. And I heard a loud voice from heaven saying, "Behold, the tabernacle of God is with men, and He will dwell with them, and they shall be His people. God Himself will be with them and be their God" (Rev.21:2,3). "And there shall be no more curse, but the throne of God and of the Lamb shall be in it, and His servants shall serve Him. They shall see His face, and His name shall be on their foreheads...And they shall reign for ever and ever" (22:3, 4).

Eternal Worship of the Godhead—"Whenever the living creatures give glory and honor and thanks to Him Who sits on the throne, Who lives for ever and ever, the twenty-four elders fall down before Him Who sits on the throne and worship Him" (Rev. 4:9, 10). "And every creature which is in heaven and on the earth...I heard saying: "Blessing and honor and glory and power be to Him Who sits on the throne, and to the Lamb forever and ever!" (5:13). "For as the new heavens and the new earth which I will make shall remain before Me," says the Lord, so shall your descendants and your name remain. And it shall come to pass that from one New Moon to another, and from one Sabbath to another, all flesh shall come to worship before Me," says the Lord" (Isa. 66:22, 23).

Reader—what more could we want or ask for?!—only that we personally will be there to enjoy it all and to join in that everlasting worship. And that this will be your personal experience and blessing, is the prayer of the writer for you.

Notes

1. Ellen G. White, *Testimonies For the Church, vol.9,* (Pacific Press Publishing Association, 1948), 12, 13.

2. Rene Noorbergen, *Ellen G. White, Prophet of Destiny* (New Canaan, Connecticut: Keats Publishing Inc.) 20, 21.

3. Ibid., 5–9.

4. Ibid., 123–125.

5. Ibid., 94–97.

6. Paul Harvey, Commentator dispatch: "Paul Harvey, Nutritionist Ahead of Her Time", *The Lima, Ohio, News*, Aug. 11, 1960, (Gen. Features Corp.).

7. Noorbergen, *Prophet of Destiny*, 96, 105–107.

8. Harvey, *Nutritionist Ahead of Her Time*, 20, 21.

9. J. Cook, *The Saturday Evening Post*, March, 1984, 40–43.

10. Noorbergen, *Prophet of Destiny*, 83, 84.

11. Ibid., 80–88.

12. Ibid., 21.

13. E. G. White, *The Great Controversy*, (Mountain View, California: Pacific Press Publishing Association, 1888), 589.

14. *The Signs of the Times Magazine*, April 21, 1890.

15. White, *The Great Controversy*, 589, 590.

16. Noorbergen, *Prophet of Destiny*, 142–145.

17. Billy Graham, *Angels: God's Secret Agents* (Doubleday and Company, Inc., 1975, Pocketbook ed.), 81, 82.

18. Billy Graham, *Peace With God*, (Montreal, P. Q.: Permabooks, Doubleday and Company, Inc., 1955) 59–65.

19. *The Muskoka Advance*, November 19, 2000.

20. Franklin M. Harold, *The Way of the Cell* (Oxford University Press, 2001), 14.

21. *The New Encyclopedia Britannica*, vol.26, (Chicago/London), 487–493.

22. *McGraw-Hill Encyclopedia of Science and Technology*, vol. 11, (New York, Washington, D. C., San Francisco), 633, 634.

23. *The Muskoka Advance*, August 22, 2004.

24. Monroe W. Strickberger, PhD., *Genetics*, (New York, London: The Macmillan Company, 1968) 542–546.

25. Ibid., 536–538.

26. Ellen G. White, *The Story of Redemption*, (Washington D. C.: Review and Herald Publishing Association, 1947), 20, 21.

27. White, *The Great Controversy*, 644, 645.

28. Strickberger, *Genetics*, 319.

29. "Radiation," *The New Encyclopedia Britannica*, 490.

30. Strickberger, *Genetics*, 551.

31. "Mutagens and Carcinogens," *McGraw-Hill Encyclopedia of Science and Technology*, 597.

32. Strickberger, *Genetics*, 818.

33. "Radioecology," *McGraw-Hill Encyclopedia of Science and Technology*, 149.

34. Strickberger, *Genetics*, 545.

35. Ellen G. White, *Selected Messages*, book 2, (Washington, D.C.: Review and Herald Publishing Association), 288.

36. Ellen G. White, *Testimonies*, vol. 6, (Washington, D.C.: Review and Herald Publishing Association), 186.

37. Ellen G. White, *Temperance*, (Mountain View, CA: Pacific Press Publishing Association), 74, 75.

38. Strickberger, *Genetics*, 515.

39. Noorbergen, *Prophet of Destiny*, 127–130.

40. Ellen G. White, *Testimonies*, vol. 1, (Mountain View, CA: Pacific Press Publishing Association) 341–343.

41. Ellen G. White, *Testimonies*, vol. 5, (Mountain View, CA: Pacific Press Publishing Association), 193.

42. Ellen G. White, *The Desire of Ages*, trade edition, (Mountain View, CA: Pacific Press Publishing Association, 1896) 318, 319.

43. Ellen G. White, *Early Writings*, (Mountain View, CA: Pacific Press Publishing Association, 1896), 184.

44. White, *The Great Controversy*, 516, 517.

45. White, *Testimonies*, vol. 1, 304.

46. Ellen G. White, *Testimonies*, vol. 3, (Washington, D.C.: Review and Herald Publishing Association), 138, 139.

47.   Ellen G. White, *Spiritual Gifts*, vol. 3 (Washington, D. C.: Review and Herald Publishing Association, reprint, 1945) 64, 75.

48.   *Christian Week*, December 17, 2004, vol.18, no. 19, (Winnipeg, MB).

49.   Ellen G. White, *Patriarchs and Prophets*, (Mountain View, CA: Pacific Press Publishing Association), 44–51.

50.   Ellen G. White, *Selected Messages*, book 1, (Washington, D.C.: Review and Herald Publishing Association), 268.

51.   Ellen G. White, *The Story of Redemption*, (Washington, D.C.: Review and Herald Publishing Association) 22.

52.   White, *Early Writings*, 18.

53.   Ellen G. White, The Desire of Ages, (Mountain View, CA: Pacific Press Publishing Association) 311.

54.   Ellen G. White, *Prophets and Kings*, (Mountain View, CA: Pacific Press Publishing Association) 586, 587.

55.   Ellen G. White, *Education*, (Mountain View, CA: Pacific Press Publishing Association) 125.

We'd love to have you download our catalog of titles we publish at:

www.TEACHServices.com

or write or email us your thoughts, reactions, or criticism about this or any other book we publish at:

TEACH Services, Inc.
254 Donovan Road
Brushton, NY 12916

info@TEACHServices.com

or you may call us at:

518/358-3494